If you are concerned with maintaining the status quo, if you are searching for ways to rationalize membership decline, if you are interested in feeding the flock but not adding to it . . . this book is *NOT* for you. It *is* for you if you want to understand just what you need to do for your church to grow to its full potential.

To: The 120 Fellowship
The Body of Christ in action

Leading Your Church to Growth

C. PETER WAGNER

The Secret of Pastor/People
Partnership in Dynamic Church Growth

MARC Europe
The British Church Growth Association

Scripture quotations in this publication are from the *New King James Version* of the Holy Bible © 1979, 1980, 1982, Thomas Nelson, Inc., Publishers. Also quoted is the *NIV, New International Version* of the Holy Bible. Copyright © 1973 and 1978 by New York International Bible Society. Used by permission. Published in the UK by Hodder & Stoughton.

British Library C.I.P.

Wagner, C. Peter
   Leading your church to growth : the secret of
   pastor/people partnership in church growth.
   1. Church growth
   I. Title
   254'.5   BV652.25

   ISBN 0–947697–22–5 (MARC Europe)
   ISBN 0–948704–00–4 (British Church Growth Association)

MARC Europe is an integral part of World Vision, an international Christian humanitarian organisation. MARC's object is to assist Christian leaders with factual information, surveys, management skills, strategic planning and other tools for evangelism. MARC also publishes and distributes related books on mission, church growth, management, spiritual maturity and other topics.

The British Church Growth Association is a coordinating body for those interested in the growth (spiritual, numerical, organic and incarnational) of the British church today. It comprises researchers, teachers, consultants and practitioners who share information, insights, experience and new thinking through regional and national activities, a regular journal, occasional publications and other resources, seminars and conferences. It is located at 59 Warrington Road, Harrow, Middlesex HA1 1SZ.

Foreword

Professor C Peter Wagner has the remarkable ability to write clearly and perceptively about issues at the top of the Church's agenda. *Leading Your Church to Growth* is yet another example of his being able to scratch the Church where it itches.

The main purpose of the book is to challenge pastors to become equippers of their congregations so that God-given goals for growth may be achieved. Wagner argues from the Scriptures and recent church history that church growth is according to the will of God. He refutes the theologians and church leaders who talk and act as if church decline is acceptable and numerical church growth is unimportant.

The challenge to grow is placed squarely before every pastor and congregation and the price to be paid for growth is spelt out. Wagner does not hesitate to call for quality leadership and membership in order to fulfil Christ's commission to 'Go to all peoples everywhere and make them my disciples' (Matthew 28:19).

If your church were to follow the counsel and teaching about the role of the pastor and leaders contained within this book, it would transform its life and ministry. Chapters 2, 3 and 4 ought to be required reading for every minister and every church council.

Wagner carefully steers us through the complex relationship between church and para-church structures. He offers insights that are particularly helpful in understanding some of the tensions caused by house groups and between the established churches and the developing House Church movement in the United Kingdom.

If your church really wants to grow, to understand its mission, and to set goals for growth, then take the prescription offered in this book. I believe that leaders who do will see their churches growing to the glory of God.

Dr Roy Pointer
Church Growth Consultant,
Bible Society

Table of Contents

Introduction

This is a book on church leadership for growth. It is intentionally a narrow book: It is not intended to be a survey of management theories as applied to the church. It is not a textbook on pastoral theology. It does not attempt to show how some organizational principle can be used in a church such as a book I have with the subtitle, "How to Realize Your Church's Potential Through a Systems Approach."

Many other books have done these things and done them well.

No, this book is about leadership narrowly focused—leadership for church membership growth. If you are concerned with maintaining the status quo, the book is not for you. If you are searching for ways to rationalize membership decline, you won't need it. If you are interested in feeding the flock but not adding to it, there are many excellent books other than this one which can help you.

I was challenged when I read a recent critique

of the Church Growth Movement. The author acknowledges that, among factors discovered in growing churches, dynamic leadership consistently shows up. But then he says that the Church Growth Movement "has done little to actually give guidance in the kind of leadership needed." He asks for more help in knowing what kind of leadership works well in what kind of situation.

This is, I think, an accurate assessment and a legitimate request. As I review the substantial body of church growth literature produced over the last decade and a half, I do not find any sustained discussion of just how and why leadership influences growth positively or negatively.[1] Strong pastoral leadership is regularly affirmed as a positive growth factor, but an in-depth analysis is yet lacking. My intention is to begin to fill that void. While this book will most certainly not be the last word on the subject, I believe it will at least open up avenues of fruitful discussion which can be further developed in the years to come.

With this as a goal, I must necessarily write for clergy and laity. Both are indispensable ingredients in the growth package, and leadership has quite different implications for each. I am going to argue for strong pastoral leadership while recognizing that this can be expressed through many different styles. I am going to make a case for intelligent followership on the part of laypeople while avoiding the extremes of passivity or subservience. Churches cannot grow vigorously without the proper combination of both. Many pastors simply do not understand their God-given leadership responsibility. But even when they discover it, many of them are not able to lead their churches into growth because the key lay leaders of the congregation have never discovered how to

work alongside a church growth pastor. I hope
and pray that God will use this book to promote
understanding and harmony between clergy and
laity, to remove unnecessary barriers to growth in
hundreds of congregations, to open the doors of
the kingdom of heaven to multitudes who have yet
to believe in Jesus, and to bring glory to Himself.

Note
1. Donald A. McGavran's section, "Administering for Church
Growth," in the 1980 revision of *Understanding Church Growth*
(Grand Rapids: Wm. B. Eerdmans Publishing Co., 1980) deals mostly
with principles of bridging, goal setting and planning, but not with
the pastor-people relationships of the local parish. Published in
the UK by S.P.C.K.

1

Why a Growing Church?

The subject is church leadership for church growth.

The obvious place to start is with church growth. Just how legitimate is it to hold up growth as a goal for the local church? If growth is either undesirable or trivial, there is little value in struggling to lead a church in that direction. That's why it is necessary, at the outset, to discuss the question: is church growth OK?

The Church Growth Movement has boldly asserted that not only is church growth OK, but it is the will of Almighty God. From the time he founded the movement in 1955, Donald McGavran of Fuller Seminary has declared with the tireless verve of a prophet that God wants His lost sheep found and brought into the fold. Those who have chosen to identify with McGavran's movement, and I include myself among them, have chosen as their biblical rallying point Jesus' Great Commission to "go therefore and make disciples of all the nations" (Matt. 28:19).

During the early years, practically all church growth research and instruction were directed toward the Third World. McGavran founded the Fuller School of World Mission in Pasadena, California in 1965 and the more than 400 graduate theses and dissertations produced since then have focused almost exclusively on the spread of the gospel in Asia, Africa, and Latin America. It was only in 1972 that initial, tentative efforts were made to see if perhaps church growth principles could be adapted to the American scene.

Many American pastors and denominational executives found the teachings of the Church Growth Movement a helpful supplement to their seminary training. Momentum picked up and continued to increase. Lyle E. Schaller, America's ranking parish consultant, in surveying the religious panorama of America[1] rated the Church Growth Movement as "the most influential development of the 1970s."

At the beginning, most of the individuals, local churches, and denominations who identified with church growth teachings were evangelicals. The Church of the Nazarene, the Evangelical Covenant Church, Southern Baptists and Missouri Synod Lutherans were among the most enthusiastic. A large body of literature has been produced. Seminaries have introduced church growth into their curricula.[2] Agencies have emerged which have packaged church growth teachings and made them available in a practical form to local parishes. Some persons have become professional church growth consultants working on both denominational and interdenominational levels.[3] To my knowledge, the first denomination to have created a national office of Church Growth Consultant is the Evangelical Covenant Church, but others have similar district and conference offices.

Through the mid-1970s most of the mainline denominations were highly suspicious of the Church Growth Movement. Books were published with titles such as *Church Growth Is Not the Point*. But as the decade came to a close, the serious decline in mainline church membership, which had begun in the 1960s, became frightening to many leaders. The trendy efforts to rationalize membership decline through theological arguments sounded more and more hollow. A National Council of Churches study looking into "What the Mainline Denominations Are Doing in Evangelism" reported that the "big news of the past triennium is that the church growth approach, originated at Fuller Seminary, has been sweeping the mainline denominations."[4] This is quoted by Richard G. Hutcheson, Jr., in his penetrating book, *Mainline Churches and the Evangelicals*. Part of the mainline reaction to church growth has been a persistent line of criticism through articles and books written, by and large, by Christian social activists who perceive the social ethics of the Church Growth Movement to be weak.[5] But, Hutcheson says, "despite the controversy, the Church Growth approach clearly has been widely adopted by the mainline churches."[6]

One of the reasons some mainline churches gave for their reticence in accepting church growth teachings was their embarrassment at admitting that institutional survival could be a legitimate priority. It took a long time for the rebellious anti-institutional social psychology of the 1960s to wear off. But now the climate is changing. The United Church of Christ, which lost over 300,000 members since 1965, recently headlined in their official publication: "Now is the time for

UCC churches to stop erosion and set goals for growth."[7] William P. Thompson, stated clerk of the United Presbyterian Church, reported to the 1982 general assembly that the previous year alone the church had lost 46,232 members. Thompson's comment: "The membership loss cannot be rationalized away . . . . It is an indictment of our lukewarm zeal in the work of the Gospel and points up weaknesses in the recruitment and meaningful involvement of new members—for which all of us bear responsibility."[8]

Is It OK Not to Grow?

Another reason why many mainline leaders were turned off to church growth was an innocent but overenthusiastic arrogance on the part of some church growth advocates. I myself was among them. In the early days we frequently said, "Any church can grow—if it wants to grow." And then the corollary: "Every church should grow—if your church is not growing you are out of the will of God." Few church growth teachers make such sweeping statements anymore. The critics have been heard. Perspectives have broadened. Attitudes have mellowed.

Across the country many smaller churches of 200 active members or less find themselves torn apart when the question of whether or not to grow is presented to them. It is more difficult for them to say yes to such a question than it is for most middle-sized or large churches. Why is this? It is because of their value system. They have placed a very high value on being a single-cell church. Carl S. Dudley, who has analyzed the dynamics of the small church as thoroughly as anyone, says, "The experience of belonging to a small congregation meets a basic human need for social order and metaphysical orderliness."⁹

Churches which have remained small for some time are not simply miniature large churches. They have a different character altogether. The major difference lies in interpersonal relationships. In the small church there are no strangers. Everyone knows everyone else. The social situation is predictable and therefore comfortable. Preserving this value by maintaining the status quo becomes a very high priority in the lives of many church members.

Carl Dudley points out that this is the major obstacle to growth in small churches. The intimacy of the small church is not an accident, it is part of its very nature. Dudley says, "The essential character of the small church is this capacity to care about people personally. The small church cannot grow in membership size without giving up its most precious appeal, its intimacy."¹⁰

Some small churches may be willing to give up their intimacy and grow but they cannot because of the social situation. They have a terminal illness. Either their community is changing radically or, as is the case in some rural areas, it is disappearing. The realistic prognosis is that the church will die. Growth potential is near zero. Churches with terminal illnesses do not need to be loaded with more guilt because they are not growing; they need to be cared for and counseled. Terminal illnesses, by the way, are not limited to small churches. They can kill middle-sized and large churches as well.

Other churches are growing by standing still. Churches which have a primary ministry in a community of extremely high mobility such as a college town or near a military base do not grow easily. It is not uncommon for such churches to see an annual attrition rate of 30 percent or more. This compares to a national average of around 7 percent. Many of these churches have excellent outreach programs; they are leading large numbers of unbelievers to Jesus Christ and folding them into the church, but year after year the church just stays about the same.

For these three kinds of churches—small churches which value their single-cell nature, terminally ill churches, and churches in areas of unusual mobility—should not be expected to grow. It is recognized that God can direct them in other avenues and bless them and use them for His glory. If God is so leading them, it's O.K. not to grow.

This book is not addressed to churches with little or no growth potential, particularly to the first two types of churches. There are many wonderfully consecrated Christian pastors who are called to serve such churches. Because of their personalities, temperaments, spiritual gift mixes, health conditions, age, family situations, or any combination of the above, they will never be church-growth pastors. I want to make it clear that God loves these pastors and so do I. I do not want anything in this book to be interpreted as a put-down of these men and women of God.

But there are thousands of pastors of non-growing churches which do have growth potential. Obstacles to their growth can be identified and removed. This book is addressed to such pastors and such churches. If, by chance, some twinges of guilt for nongrowth occur here and there in situations where growth potential exists, I will not be disappointed. I will even suggest that it might be interpreted as a nudge from the Holy Spirit Himself. Why? Because, with certain important exceptions as I have mentioned, church growth is the will of God. Let me elaborate.

Church Growth and the Will of God

The Bible is in favor of church growth. Theologians affirm that the central purpose of Jesus' coming to earth was to die on the cross for the redemption of humankind. The cross, accompanied by the resurrection, is the central point of world history. Jesus Himself said, "The Son of Man has come to seek and to save that which was lost" (Luke 19:10). Who are the lost? They are obviously the people in the world who have yet to hear and accept the good news that Jesus, on the cross, died for their sins. When they believe that and acknowledge Jesus as Saviour and Lord, they are reconciled to God once again and no longer lost. It is summed up in John 3:16: "For God so loved the world that He gave His only begotten Son, that whoever believes in Him should not perish but have everlasting life."

How is the good news of salvation through Jesus Christ to be communicated to the lost? Jesus Himself is not doing it, nor will He. He has chosen to delegate that responsibility to His followers. At one point He compared the lost people of the world to harvest fields and commanded His disciples to "pray the Lord of the harvest to send out laborers into His harvest" (Matt. 9:38). God is the one who ripens the harvest as the apostle Paul acknowledges: "I have planted, Apollos watered, but God gave the increase" (1 Cor. 3:6). But while God *ripens* the harvest, He does not *reap* the harvest. He expects us to be His agents in reaping.

This is an awesome responsibility. Jesus said to His disciples, "If you forgive the sins of any, they are forgiven them; and if you retain the sins of any, they are retained" (John 20:23). Volumes in theological libraries have been written on this, but one thing is clear. If we human beings don't carry the gospel message to the lost they will remain lost. As Romans says, "How shall they hear without a preacher? . . . How beautiful are the feet of those who preach the gospel of peace" (Rom. 10:14-15).

It is with this in mind that Jesus gave His very last command to His followers. He came to earth, lived a sinless life, taught His disciples, was executed on the cross, rose from the dead, and appeared again to His disciples for forty days. After all of this, the last thing He said before He was taken up into a cloud was: "You shall receive power when the Holy Spirit has come upon you; and you will be witnesses to Me in Jerusalem, and in all Judea and in Samaria, and to the end of the earth" (Acts 1:8). If we fail to take seriously this Great Commission we have missed the central point of historic Christianity.

What God expects of us in fulfilling the Great Commission is more clearly detailed in the closing words of Matthew. "Go therefore and make disciples of all the nations, baptizing them in the name of the Father and of the Son and of the Holy Spirit, teaching them to observe all things that I have commanded you" (Matt. 28:19-20). Three of the action verbs in this statement are participles in the original Greek: *go, baptize,* and *teach.* The one imperative is *make disciples.* This is God's expectation for those of us who are His followers today: to see that every possible lost person in the world becomes a disciple of Jesus Christ.

How, then, is a disciple to be recognized? Obviously, it is a person who has turned from an old way of life and acknowledged Jesus as Lord and

Saviour. But just a verbal affirmation of faith is not enough. Jesus said, "You will know them by their fruits" (Matt. 7:16). There are many fruits that are borne in the life of a true Christian through the Holy Spirit. However, the fruit that the Church Growth Movement has selected as the validating criterion for discipleship is responsible church membership. This choice may be somewhat arbitrary, but not entirely. Jesus at another point in His ministry announced the purpose of His coming by declaring that "I will build My church" (Matt. 16:18). The church is called the Body of Christ. It is the bride of Christ. It is near and dear to the heart of God. Commitment to Christ is somehow incomplete without a simultaneous commitment to the Body of Christ, the church.

Evangelism is not only reaching people with the gospel message and bringing them to a decision for Christ, it is making them disciples. My favorite definition of evangelism is the one developed by the Anglican Archbishops in 1918: "To evangelize is so to present Christ Jesus in the power of the Holy Spirit that men and women shall come to put their trust in God through Him, to accept Him as their Saviour, and serve Him as their King in the fellowship of His Church." This ties commitment to Christ with commitment to the church.

God's will is clear. He does not desire that "any should perish but that all should come to repentance" (2 Pet. 3:9). He wants men and women everywhere to come to Him and into the church of Jesus Christ. In short, it is God's will that churches grow.

A model church in the New Testament is the one in Jerusalem which was founded on the day of

Pentecost. On that one day the nucleus of 120 added 3,000 new members. They were baptized, they grew in their understanding of Christian doctrine, they worshiped together regularly, they developed fellowship groups, they shared their material goods with one another, they exercised their spiritual gifts. As a result the church continued to grow and "the Lord added to the church daily those who were being saved" (Acts 2:47). This was a healthy church. And one characteristic of healthy churches is that they grow.

What About the Numbers Game?

Some say they do not buy into church growth because they do not want to play the "numbers game." They feel that church growth is overly concerned with gathering statistics, drawing graphs of growth, calculating decadal growth rates, comparing the performance of one church with another, and setting measurable goals for growth. Some have been so upset by this that they have labeled church growth "numerolatry."

I was in a discussion group a while ago, and a person in the group was hung up against numbers. At one point in the discussion he exclaimed, "My Bible tells me to *feed* the sheep, not to *count* them!" I didn't answer at the time, but later I was reading Phillip Keller's book *A Shepherd Looks at Psalm 23.* Keller is a professional sheep rancher who is also a sensitive Christian author. Keller has a great deal to say about feeding the sheep. But he also explains that it is "so essential for a careful shepherd to look over his flock every day, *counting* them to see that all are able to be up and on their feet."[11] He tells of what a great blessing it is when a ewe has *twin* lambs instead of only one. I believe that counting sheep is such a natural part of the shepherd's life that Jesus took for granted His followers would know that. It is biblical to feed the sheep, but also to count them.

God Himself does a lot of counting. He even has the hairs on each person's head numbered. When each individual comes to faith in Jesus Christ, that name is written in the Lamb's book of life. Even the littlest person is important in heaven and gets individual recognition. There is joy in heaven over *one* sinner who repents (Luke 15:7), so somebody up there must be keeping close track.

As I see it, those who object to numbers are usually trying to avoid superficiality in Christian commitment. I agree with this. I am not interested in names on church rolls. There are already too many nominal, inactive and non-resident church members in America. I am not interested in churches which are religious social clubs. I am not interested in decisions for Christ totaled up as people raise their hands or come forward after a crusade. I am not interested in Christians who profess faith in Christ but do not demonstrate it in their lives. These numbers are unimportant.

But I am vitally interested in lost men and women who put their faith in Jesus Christ and are born again. I am interested in true disciples who take up their cross daily to follow Jesus. I am interested in kingdom people who relate to Jesus as their Lord. I am interested in Spirit-filled people who have experienced the power of the Holy Spirit and are using their spiritual gifts. I am interested in responsible church members who continue "steadfastly in the apostles' doctrine and fellowship, in breaking of bread, and in prayers" (Acts 2:42) as did believers in the Jerusalem church.

When numbers represent these kinds of people, they are much more than a "numbers game."

They become a game of life and death, a game of time or eternity. The stakes are the highest in the world, for "he who has the Son has life; he who does not have the Son of God does not have life" (1 John 5:12).

Church Members Are Not Enough

Quantity is not enough without corresponding quality. But quality is not self-explanatory.

All too often I run up against a person who says, "Our church is interested in quality, not in quantity." I would rather hear the person say, "Our church is interested in quality *as well as* quantity." With the latter statement I can heartily agree, but I do not believe we need to set quality over against quantity. We can and should have both.

There are at least two substantial issues involved in a discussion of church quality. One is the matter of a measuring instrument and the other relates to the possibility of psychological screening out.

Over here we might observe a church which is growing vigorously. A neighboring pastor says, "Oh, yes, so-and-so is getting growth, but I have some questions about it. Is he really preaching the *gospel*? Is the net result really a *church*?" I have heard comments like this on numerous occasions.

One of the serious problems involved in questioning the quality of a particular church is that, given the state of the art, such questions must by nature remain unanswered. At present we have no measuring instrument that is accepted both by the person who asks the question and the person the question is asked about. Up to now we may have been able to compare the quality of two churches which have the same philosophy of ministry or to compare this year's quality of a given church with last year's. But even there we have been severely limited in what we can do.

Everyone has an idea as to what constitutes high quality in a church. Pentecostal churches will measure what percentage of their members have been baptized in the Holy Spirit and spoken in tongues. Southern Baptists don't agree. They measure Sunday School enrollment. Episcopalians don't agree. They measure how many take communion. Quakers don't agree. They measure how many stand up for non-violence. Seventh-Day Adventists measure tithers. Lutherans drink beer and fight for doctrinal purity. Fundamentalist Baptists fight for doctrinal purity but don't drink beer. Presbyterians believe that sanctification is a never-ending process, while Nazarenes believe it can be sudden and total.[12]

To attempt to bring order into the picture, Richard L. Gorsuch of the Fuller Seminary School of Psychology and I have teamed up to work on developing an appropriate measuring instrument for church quality. We need one which will be accepted interdenominationally and internationally. It has to be simple enough for any pastor to use without the aid of a computer. We have made a modest beginning, but a great deal more remains to be done. The findings of the first phase of the research were published in *Leadership* journal which is also cooperating in the effort.

A survey of hundreds of pastors has allowed us to compile a preliminary list of measurable quality factors in the life of a congregation in ranking order. The twelve factors are:

1. *Bible knowledge.* Church members are increasing in their grasp of the teachings of the Bible. They can integrate this with a theological

system that enables them to apply the Bible's teachings to their life situation.

2. *Personal devotions.* Members spend time daily in prayer, Bible reading, meditation, and other personal spiritual exercises.

3. *Worship.* Members regularly participate in the worship services scheduled by the church.

4. *Witnessing.* Members regularly attempt to share their faith in Jesus Christ with unbelievers.

5. *Lay ministry.* The lay people of the church are engaged in such ministries as teaching and discipling. In some cases this happens through consciously discovering, developing, and using their spiritual gifts.

6. *Missions.* The church actively supports missions, organizing and sustaining a strong program for recruiting, sending, and financing home and foreign missionaries.

7. *Giving.* Members give an appropriate portion of their income to the local church and/or to other Christian causes.

8. *Fellowship.* Members are growing in their personal relationships with each other through regular participation in church fellowship groups of one kind or another.

9. *Distinctive life-style.* Members generally manifest their faith in Christ by living a life-style clearly and noticeably distinct from that of non-Christians in the same community.

10. *Attitude toward religion.* Church members regard their involvement in the church primarily as a service to God rather than a means to fulfill personal needs.

11. *Social service.* Members are serving others outside the congregation. This includes direct personal involvement with the poor and needy, or in programs designed to help the needy.

12. *Social justice.* Either through the congregation as a whole or through specialized Christian agencies, members are striving to make changes in sociopolitical structures that will contribute to a more moral and just society.

How to measure each one, how to weigh the results, and how to rank a church on a scale, say, of 1 to 100 is the problem we are working on. At best it will probably take several years to develop a measuring instrument and field test it sufficiently. Meanwhile questions of church quality will probably have to remain moot.

Some pastors use the question of quality as a device for psychological screening out. Despite what they say, they are not really seeking an objective measurement of church quality. What they are seeking is personal self-esteem.

The self-image of a congregation is frequently transferred to the pastor. A small, dormant church with low self-esteem as a congregation will likely have a pastor who feels the same way. The pastor, naturally, needs affirmation. Affirmation could come through growth, but the church is not growing nor is it expected to. If self-esteem can't come through a growth (quantity), how can it come?

Through quality! But what is quality in such a case? It is comfort—a loving, personal, upbuilding relationship with the people in the church. This is not something objective and measurable, it is something felt and enjoyed.

If the above description is accurate, I would expect that some of the pastors now raising the "quality not quantity" banner will also resist attempts to objectify and measure church quality. There is too much risk involved. Suppose the growing church came out higher on the quality scale? Self-esteem could take a beating.

Whether the issues of church quality arise from the objective desire for accurate measurement or from a subjective need for a psychological cushion, we are taking them seriously. Church growth believes not only in churches but in high quality churches, churches which bring glory to their chief Shepherd, Jesus Christ. Growing churches are growing in quality as well as quantity.

The Cultural Mandate Is Important

Part of a high quality church is to be significantly involved in ministry to the poor and downtrodden. Christian social responsibility cannot be neglected. Too often in the recent past, evangelical churches especially have been negligent in this area of their duty.

As I see the total mission of the church, God has given us both an evangelistic mandate and a cultural mandate. I have previously discussed the evangelistic mandate without using the term when I mentioned Jesus' Great Commission and our obligation to make disciples of all nations. Saving souls is the first step but it is not enough. Concern for the whole person is essential. Loving your neighbor as yourself means becoming involved with people's health, welfare and human dignity.

John the Baptist, Jesus, Paul and the other apostles preached the Kingdom of God. The kingdom they preached is both future and present. Its fullness is future—there will be no sin, sickness, poverty, demon possession, tears, oppression, or death. In the present, however, there is a mixture. The powers of evil are still active. Satan, like a roaring lion, is seeking whom he may devour. Christians, for whom Jesus is King, are citizens of the Kingdom of God and their lives are expected to reflect the values of God's kingdom. Furthermore, the churches in which they gather together should also reflect the life-style of the kingdom.

The first responsibility of Christians in this present age is to get as many people as possible into the kingdom and under the lordship of Jesus Christ. This comes through the new birth. The words of Jesus come to us clearly: "Most assuredly, I say to you, unless one is born again, he cannot see the kingdom of God" (John 3:3). Guiding new people into the kingdom is the evangelistic mandate.

The cultural mandate is directed toward both believers and unbelievers. It is not God's will that people be poor, sick, oppressed, or demon possessed. But many are, and Christians need to be concerned. They need to take kingdom-oriented action. This is the cultural mandate, and it is not optional for faithful servants of God.

As I see it, involvement in the cultural mandate occurs on two levels, which can be called, for the sake of distinction, the natural level and the supernatural level.

The natural level involves the use of everyday means such as economic resources, social change mechanisms, medical science, political power, education, psychology, and the like. It is the kind of ministry which took place on the Jericho Road when the Good Samaritan found the man who had fallen victim to thieves. He treated the wounds, made him comfortable in the inn, and prepaid his food and lodging. It is the kind of ministry that God directed Zacchaeus to. He gave half his goods to the poor and paid back four times what he had cheated people out of. It is the kind of ministry the Old Testament prophets spoke about when they denounced rulers who favored the rich and neglected the poor.

American Christians are fulfilling the cultural mandate on the natural level somewhat, but not nearly as much as they should. Organizations such as World Vision, World Relief, Voice of Calvary, and Evangelicals for Social Action are helping greatly. The collective conscience for social ministries is rising. In June, 1982, a high-level consultation met in Grand Rapids, Michigan. Called the Consultation on the Relationship between Evangelism and Social Responsibility, the group drew up a strong declaration favoring increased activities in relief, development, and legislation for justice.

The second, or supernatural, level for fulfilling the cultural mandate involves the direct power of the Holy Spirit for healings, deliverance, and miracles. When Jesus sent out His twelve apostles the first time, He gave them clear directions as to what they were to say and what they were to do. They were to say, "The kingdom of heaven is at hand" (Matt. 10:7). But actions speak louder than words. Here is what they were to do: "Heal the sick, cleanse the lepers, raise the dead, cast out demons" (Matt. 10:8). Notice that Jesus did not expect them to start clinics or leprosariums, which are fine on the natural level and should be encouraged. No, this was something entirely different where the power of the Holy Spirit is activated in a direct way through the citizens of the kingdom of heaven.

For many years I thought that such activity had terminated with the apostolic age and that today we were limited to fulfilling the cultural mandate through natural means. More recently, however, I have done a 180-degree turn. Abundant biblical and experiential evidence has now thoroughly convinced me that Jesus truly is the same yesterday, today, and forever. I now take literally His words, "Most assuredly, I say to you, he who believes in Me, the works that I do he will do also; and greater works than these he will do, because I go to My Father" (John 14:12). The Pentecostals and the charismatics have known this for some time, but many of us who have not personally identified with either of those movements are now beginning to understand something of what they are talking about. Fuller Seminary is pioneering some academic activity on this level with a course begun by John Wimber in 1982 entitled "MC510 Signs, Wonders and Church Growth."[13] I myself am engaged in researching the worldwide relationship between supernatural signs and wonders and the growth of the church, and finding that the gospel is actually spreading today as it was in the days of the apostles who "went out and preached everywhere, the Lord working with them and confirming the word through the accompanying signs" (Mark 16:20).

Halting Twenty Years of Church Decline

One of the major research reports on American churches in recent years begins with these words: "An unprecedented period in the life of the North American church began in the mid-1960s. For the first time since records allow us to recall, many major denominations actually stopped growing in membership and began to decline, and the growth rate of most others slowed considerably."[14]

In the ten-year period from 1965 to 1975 the Episcopal church lost 17 percent of its membership or 575,000 persons. The United Presbyterians lost 12 percent or 375,000 members. The

United Methodists lost 10 percent or 1,100,000 members, and so on. While this was going on, some of their leaders were proclaiming, "People are leaving the church. It could not be a better sign."[15] The expectation was that those who were leaving were the low quality Christians and that soon the churches would be pared down like Gideon's army and begin to grow again. But what worked at Midian did not seem to work in Minneapolis. The decline has continued and most leaders no longer think it is a good sign at all.

Analyzing the reasons for the decline is no small task. Some researchers have argued that contextual factors are the main cause. Contextual factors include demographic shifts, socioeconomic fluctuations, and gradual changes in American cultural patterns.[16] While contextual factors are certainly important, my personal conclusion is that probably institutional factors are even more important. Institutional factors are those which can be controlled by the churches themselves. They are both local and national. *Local* institutional factors can be controlled by the individual congregations and the main thrust of this book— church leadership and church growth—deals with them. *National* institutional factors have to do with policies established by denominational agencies and which affect all the churches in the jurisdiction.

A major reason for leaning toward institutional factors as the principal cause of mainline church decline is the fact that in the same country at the same time (in other words, holding contextual factors constant) many evangelical denominations were growing vigorously. In the 1965-1975 period while the United Methodists *lost* over one million members, the Southern Baptists *gained* over one million members. The Church of God (Cleveland) gained by 67 percent, the Assemblies of God gained 33 percent, and the Church of the Nazarene gained 29 percent. I see two principal institutional factors which help explain the phenomenon:

First, the legacy of liberal theology. Beginning with the rise of the social gospel movement toward the end of the last century, the mainline denominations embraced, to one degree or another, liberal theology. Liberal theology inevitably tends to dull the cutting edge of evangelism and church planting. At least one denominational study of membership decline indicated that their losses were coming not so much from current members who were deciding to leave the denomination, as from the failure of the churches to win new people to Christ and plant new churches.[17] At least three other studies, all done by mainline insiders, have shown a negative correlation of liberalism with membership growth and a positive correlation of theological conservatism.[18]

Second, priority shifts in denominational bureaucracies. Shifting priorities is, generally speaking, an outcome of liberal theology. While recognizing that the mission of the church includes both the evangelistic and the cultural mandates, traditionally American Christians in virtually all denominations have given priority to the evangelistic mandate. But, through the years, liberalism has tended to reduce the urgency of evangelism, in some cases even questioning whether Muslims, for example, should really be persuaded to become disciples of Jesus Christ. Presbyterian Richard G. Hutcheson, Jr., sees the issues vividly. He points out that while evangelicals have always been clear as to what evangelism means, liberals for years have been attempting to work out alternate definitions which refuse to identify evangelism with soul winning. Hutcheson says, "The liberals know very well what the evangelicals mean by the term, and such a narrowly limited meaning is exactly what they are trying to avoid!"[19]

The trend had been building for decades, but it came to a head in the tumultuous decade of the sixties. Social pressures arising from the civil rights movement, the anti-war movement, the hippie countercultural movement, the death of God movement, and the new morality influenced many mainline bureaucracies to prioritize the cultural mandate over the evangelistic mandate. One of the inevitable results was the twenty-year period of church decline. The evangelical denominations did not switch priorities because their strong conservative theological base would not allow them to do it.

My own perception is that the trends are beginning to move in the other direction. I lack empirical evidence for this, and confess that perhaps my own hopes are being interpreted as realities. But my heart is for church growth, not church decline. I would love to see membership declines in the mainline denominations bottom out and begin to soar upward. But I am afraid that they will not unless and until the evangelistic mandate is restored to its biblical position as the top priority. I am not suggesting a reduction in social ministry, simply an increase in soul-winning evangelism and new church planting. Liberal stalwarts will fight against this, but they need not prevail.

The Vital Signs of a Healthy Church

If institutional factors are as important as I

think they are in church growth, it will be helpful to identify some of them specifically. A few years ago I listed what I called the seven vital signs of a healthy church derived from my studies of growing churches in America. They were published in a book called *Your Church Can Grow* (Regal Books). The seven signs have since been scrutinized very carefully. They have been addressed in many books, articles, and papers, and at least four computer-based tests have been run on them. The most accessible of these studies is a book entitled *Turning the Tide* by Pastor Paul Beasley-Murray and Professor Alan Wilkinson, published in 1981 by the British Bible Society in London. It tests the vital signs on British Baptist churches with memberships in excess of fifty. The others are unpublished graduate theses.

By and large, the seven vital signs have held up and have been found helpful for many church leaders who are involved in planning for growth in their churches. None has actually been contradicted, although tests for one or two have come up inconclusive. Perhaps a brief summary and updating of the vital signs will help to establish the context for what follows in this book.

1. *A pastor who is a possibility thinker and whose dynamic leadership has been used to catalyze the entire church into action for growth.* The rest of this book is an elaboration on this first vital sign. Over the years its importance has been reinforced by feedback from the field more than any of the others. Only one significant voice has questioned it, that of a church leader I greatly admire, Lyle E. Schaller. Schaller says he does not see himself as a part of the Church Growth Movement, but "I have no difficulty with 97 percent of what they say." Apparently part of that other 3 per-

cent is the role of the pastor. He says, "I think the church growth movement overstates the importance of the minister in terms of church growth."[20]

This surprises me because my research has led me in exactly the opposite direction, and the next two chapters will explain my point of view. The findings of Beasley-Murray and Wilkinson "broadly support Wagner's premise that the pastor should be a possibility thinker and a dynamic leader for growth."[21]

2. *A well-mobilized laity which has discovered, has developed, and is using all the spiritual gifts for growth.* While affirming the importance of pastoral leadership, Beasley-Murray and Wilkinson go on to say that perhaps it is even more important that the pastor of a growing church "should have a willingness or ability to delegate or share his responsibilities with the members of his fellowship. There is a fruitful interdependence which neither party can achieve on its own."[22] I couldn't agree more. That is why I have targeted this book to clergy and laity. In *Your Church Can Grow* I stress the value of spiritual gifts for lay involvement, and I will bring this up again as we move on. But my research has uncovered much more information on the importance of lay followership and I will need to develop this in some detail in later chapters.

3. *A church big enough to provide the range of services that meet the needs and expectations of its members.* I am under constant pressure to declare some optimum numerical size for a church. This I cannot do, because the optimum size of any given church depends on its own philosophy of ministry. I do not believe that every church needs to be a big church or that bigger is better. But I do believe that church leaders, under

God, need to make conscious and intelligent
choices as to the size God wants them to be and
then make their plans accordingly. It is much
clearer to me now than it was a few years ago as to
how this kind of planning is done. Later on I will
include a substantial section on what "philosophy
of ministry" means and how you can develop one
for your church.

4. *The proper balance of the dynamic relationship between celebration, congregation, and
cell.* Of all the vital signs, I think this one needs
the most updating because it was overgeneralized.
The formation of dynamic fellowship groups
within the church is a key growth factor, but there
are many ways to do it. What works in one church
may not be functional in another. I plan to elaborate on this when I revise *Your Church Can Grow.*

5. *A membership drawn primarily from one
homogeneous unit.* Through the years the homogeneous unit principle has continued to be by far
the most controversial of all church growth principles. Many were worried that it would produce racist and segregationist churches. This has not hap-
pened, however, and opposition has notably
lessened over the last couple of years. One reason
for this is the realization on the part of the mainline church leaders, who were among the most
critical, that if they are going to evangelize ethnic
America they are going to have to promote and
strengthen ethnic minority churches. One of the
major mainline affirmations of the homogeneous
unit principle appears in an official series of
United Methodist publications called "Into Our
Third Century" edited by Ezra Earl Jones. In his
contribution to the series, *Shaping the Congregation* (Abingdon Press, 1981), Methodist leader
Robert L. Wilson describes the teachings of the

Church Growth Movement. He then admits that "the membership of a typical Protestant congregation will be characterized by a high degree of homogeneity," determined, among other things, by "a number of social characteristics such as education, income, cultural level, and life-style—factors that tend to be associated with social class." While this is patently true, Wilson observes that "church leaders, particularly the clergy, find this uncomfortable." However Wilson goes on to illustrate how nearby churches of the same denomination but of different homogeneous units can be vital and meaningful groups, not at all inclined toward merger.[23] As America comes to terms with cultural pluralism and gets rid of the melting pot social psychology, I foresee a notable cooling off of the homogeneous unit principle debate.

6. *Evangelistic methods that have proved to make disciples.* This vital sign is a truism. If a church is growing it is by definition attracting new members. Studies should be made, however, to determine what percentage of the new members come from biological growth (children of families who are already church members), transfer growth (attracting those who are already Christians), or conversion growth (reaching the unchurched). While biological growth requires internal evangelism, only conversion growth requires external evangelism. It is at this point that selecting the right evangelistic method will make all the difference. Despite some advertising to the contrary, there is no single evangelistic program that is applicable to all churches, so an important ingredient in planning for church growth is an intelligent choice of an evangelistic methodology that fits your particular church.

7. *Priorities arranged in biblical order.* When I

discussed the relationship of the evangelistic mandate to the cultural mandate a few pages back I was dealing with this vital sign. This is also the main theme of a recent book of mine, *Church Growth and the Whole Gospel* (Harper & Row Publishers, 1981).

While the other vital signs of a healthy church will be mentioned here and there in passing, the main thrust of this book is to elaborate on the first two: the ways that the pastor and the people work together to lead their church to growth.

Notes

1. Lyle E. Schaller in the foreword to Donald McGavran and George G. Hunter III, *Church Growth Strategies That Work* (Nashville: Abingdon Press, 1980), p. 7.

2. A key center for professional-level training in church growth is the Fuller Seminary Doctor of Ministry program which accepts 120-150 pastors and denominational executives annually into its Church Growth I course. For more information write Fuller Seminary, 135 N. Oakland Avenue, Pasadena, California 91101.

3. Professional-level training for church growth consultation is offered by Charles E. Fuller Institute of Evangelism and Church Growth, Box 91990, Pasadena, California 91109-1990.

4. Alfred C. Krass, "What the Mainline Denominations Are Doing in Evangelism," *Christian Century*, May 2, 1979, p. 49.

5. I attempted to address the issues raised by these critics in *Church Growth and the Whole Gospel* (San Francisco: Harper & Row Publishers, 1981).

6. Richard C. Hutcheson, Jr., *Mainline Churches and the Evangelicals* (Atlanta: John Knox Press, 1981), p. 122.

7. Robert L. Burt, "Our Churches Will Grow," *A.D. United Church of Christ*, September 1982, p. 20.

8. J. Martin Bailey, "How Your Church Can Grow," *A.D. United Presbyterian*, September 1982, p. 19.

9. Carl S. Dudley, *Making the Small Church Effective* (Nashville: Abingdon Press, 1978), p. 38.

10. Ibid., p. 49.

11. Phillip Keller, *A Shepherd Looks at Psalm 23* (Grand Rapids: Zondervan Publishing House, 1970), p. 60. Published in the UK by Pickering and Inglis.

12. See C. Peter Wagner and Richard L. Gorsuch, "The Quality Church," *Leadership*, Winter 1983, p. 28.

13. For detailed information on this course see *Signs and Wonders Today*, a study guide available at $4.95 plus $1.00 postage and handling from *Christian Life*, 396 E. St. Charles Rd., Wheaton, IL 60187.

14. Dean R. Hoge and David A. Roozen, eds., *Understanding Church Growth and Decline 1950-1978* (New York: Pilgrim Press, 1979), p. 17.

15. Robert K. Hudnut, *Church Growth Is Not the Point* (New York: Harper & Row Publishers, 1975), p. xi.

16. See, for example, Dean R. Hoge, "A Test of Denominational Growth and Decline," *Understanding Church Growth and Decline*, Hoge and Roozen, eds., pp. 196-197.

17. Warren J. Hartman, *Membership Trends: A Study of Decline and Growth in the United Methodist Church 1949-1975* (Nashville: Discipleship Resources, 1976).

18. Dean M. Kelly, *Why Conservative Churches Are Growing* (New York: Harper & Row Publishers), 1972; Hoge, "A Test of Theories," p. 191; and William J. McKinney, Jr., "Performance of United Church of Christ Congregations in Massachusetts and Pennsylvania," *Understanding Church Growth and Decline*, Hoge and Roozen, eds., p. 241.

19. Hutcheson, *Mainline Churches*, p. 117.

20. "The Changing Focus of Church Finances," interview with Lyle E. Schaller, *Leadership*, Spring 1981, pp. 23-24.

21. Paul Beasley-Murray and Alan Wilkinson, *Turning the Tide: An Assessment of Baptist Church Growth in England* (London: Bible Society, 1981), p. 38.

22. Ibid.

23. Robert L. Wilson, *Shaping the Congregation* (Nashville: Abingdon Press, 1981), pp. 52-55.

2

Church Growth Is Not Cheap

It is one thing to be convinced that church growth is all right. It is quite another to see it actually occur. Church growth is usually not automatic. It takes doing. The major purpose of this book is to help you, as a church leader, understand as thoroughly as possible just what you need to do if your church is going to grow to its full potential.

True, there are some rare situations where the harvest is so ripe that churches will grow almost no matter what. Pastors of those churches seem to break all the rules, ignore church growth principles, and still see their churches boom. I do not meet many such pastors because they typically don't show up at my church growth seminars. I don't blame them. Rather than expecting them to come to me, as much as possible I go to them. If their church is growing, some church growth principles must be at work, and it is through pastors who do the right things by intuition in favorable circumstances that many new church growth principles are discovered.

There is a difference between church growth pastors and pastors of growing churches. Church growth is a technical term which describes a well-defined field of study. The term was coined by Donald A. McGavran in the 1950s when he was a missionary to India. He established the Institute of Church Growth in 1961 in Eugene, Oregon, and brought it to Pasadena, California in 1965 when he founded the Fuller Seminary School of World Mission and Institute of Church Growth. There he wrote the standard textbook in the field, *Understanding Church Growth* (Wm. B. Eerdmans Publishing Co.), first published in 1970 and revised in 1980. What is now known as the Church Growth Movement developed from there with its books, periodicals, academic programs, films, consultations services, seminars and workshops, marketing agencies, and action plans. But the target of the Church Growth Movement goes beyond all those things to pastors and lay leaders of local churches. Why? Simply because that's where church growth takes place.

Pastors who find the church growth input most helpful are those whose churches are not growing well and who need some assistance to get off dead center. Joining them are some pastors of churches which are growing but who want to make sure that some growth barrier won't surprise them down the road and cause them to lose their growth momentum. A substantial number of such leaders have studied church growth principles and applied them to their own local church situations. Many of their churches have grown and I have large files of letters and testimonies from those church growth pastors. Other churches, I am painfully aware, have not grown even with church growth principles. Church growth is not some magic formula which can produce growth in any church at any time. It is just a collection of common-sense ideas that seem to track well with biblical principles which are focused on attempting to fulfill the Great Commission more effectively than ever before. The principles, I am glad to report, are usually helpful.

Until recently I could not even guess how many church growth principles had been set forth in the field. But a recent study by John Vaughan suggests that there are 146. Donald McGavran, he calculates, has articulated 67, Peter Wagner 51 and Win Arn 28.[1] In the study itself, Vaughan lists and elaborates on 49 of the principles. How accurate his figures are I really don't know, but no one I am aware of has challenged them.

Whatever the number I am sure of one thing. Every church growth principle has exceptions. Some church leaders are so accustomed to thinking in categories of true-false or right-wrong that they mistakenly place church growth principles in those frameworks. This is one reason why the homogeneous unit principle, for example, has offended many people. They have understood church growth leaders to say that homogeneous churches are the right and true way for churches to grow, when they haven't been saying this at all. They have simply been describing the observable fact that, worldwide, most unchurched men and women are first attracted to Christ by hearing the gospel from those who talk like them, think like them, and act like them. Apparently God has been using such culturally-relevant channels of communication for the spread of the gospel for centuries, just as a matter of history. McGavran calls those channels "bridges of God." But he has never suggested that a church be kept homogeneous as a matter of doctrine or ethics. His ideal and mine is a church where lines of class, race, and language are completely broken down.

Are there exceptions to the homogeneous unit principle? Of course there are. Are there exceptions to the seven vital signs of a healthy church? Certainly.

But while each rule has its exceptions, some rules obviously have fewer exceptions than others. The two church growth principles that this book chiefly deals with are among those which have relatively few exceptions. They are:

First, the pastor must want the church to grow and be willing to pay the price.

Second, the people must want the church to grow and be willing to pay the price.

Don't all pastors want their churches to grow? Strange as it may seem, the answer is no. A nationwide survey was taken by Larry Richards a few years ago. A computer randomly selected 5,000 pastors across denominational lines. They were asked to prioritize "the greatest needs in strengthening the life and program of your church." Richards reports what he considers a surprising result: less than half of the pastors gave high priority to "planning and implementing church growth."[2] Rather than growth, their priorities were centered on maintenance. Many pastors feel that making the existing church members more comfortable is of higher importance than reaching the lost for Jesus Christ.

I also suspect that many pastors do not want their churches to grow because they are not willing to pay the price. Church growth is not cheap. It frequently requires changes in the status quo that are exceedingly uncomfortable for pastors, and as a result it is given a low priority.

Don't all members of American congregations want their churches to grow? The answer again is no. When the United Presbyterian church began to become concerned about its membership loss a few years ago, the general assembly commissioned a Special Task Force on Church Membership Trends. In his report, the chairperson of the task force, C. Edward Brubaker, said, "One theme that really stared out at us is that we United Presbyterians have not grown because we just don't care about growing." As is the case with many pastors, the people also gave low priority to reaching out to the lost. Brubaker's report says, "When we asked churches about 21 different aspects of their program, evangelism came out absolutely at the bottom of the list as to importance and time received in the church program."[3]

Why don't people want their church to grow? They are comfortable the way they are. There are some special prices that laypeople must pay for the growth of their church, and many simply are not willing to pay those costs.

While both the pastor and the people must want their church to grow and be willing to pay the price, the order is significant. With few exceptions, the pastor must be motivated for growth first, and then the people. Only in very rare cases will the people become motivated and then get the pastor excited about growth.

Some years ago I used to do field consultation with the Fuller Institute for Evangelism and Church Growth. One day I received a call from a man who identified himself as a United Methodist insurance executive. I could tell by his voice that he was an older man. He said, "I understand you people can help sick churches." I told him that we could help some, but not others. "I have been a member of my church for twenty years," he said. "I love my church, but it's dying. If you can help my church I'll pay you anything you want!" I could tell he was desperate so I encouraged him to talk about his church. He laid out his dream for the future. It sounded good. Then I asked him what his pastor thought of his dream. "That might be the problem," he said. "The pastor doesn't agree with me." I explained that it was a serious problem, and that unless the pastor changed his mind or they got another pastor there was no way I knew to help the church.

If the price for growth is so frequently too high either for the pastor or for the people, it is necessary to understand exactly what that price involves. Let's look at both sides one at a time.

The Pastor's Price for Growth

I am going to suggest five special prices that a church growth pastor must pay to lead a church to growth. I feel that it is good to get these out into the open honestly. At each of the points I have seen pastors turn back and away from growth. Jesus said, "Which of you, intending to build a tower, does not sit down first and count the cost?" (Luke 14:28). Since church growth is not cheap, pastors must ask themselves, before making plans for growth, "Am I willing to pay the price?"

Assuming the responsibility for growth

Make no mistake about it. Most church growth starts with the pastor. I agree with Dewayne Davenport who says, "If called upon to name the *key* to church growth, it would be leadership."[4] This is an awesome responsibility, and it is one which many pastors shy away from. There are three major reasons why some pastors are not willing to pay this price.

The first is that *assuming responsibility for growth involves a substantial risk—the risk of failure*. I have noticed that many pastors want someone besides themselves to be responsible for the growth of their church. They may say that "the congregation is responsible" or "the deacons are responsible" or "the session is responsible" or even "God is responsible." Some will go so far as to theologize this and convince themselves that there is Christian virtue in not assuming responsibility for growth.

The fear of failure is a tremendous psychological obstacle to some pastors. Their temperament is such that taking leadership for growth is too high a price for them to pay. I would hasten to say that there is nothing wrong with this. God has made us all with different personalities and temperaments. If a pastor cannot face the risk of failure, it would be well to decide to be a small church, non-growth pastor and to be comfortable in that role. Most churches are small churches. Some have little or no growth potential. They are holding operations. There is a need for many pastors who are willing to pastor such churches with personal satisfaction, and not with a constant feeling of frustration and guilt that their church is not growing as vigorously as some.

The second reason why many pastors are not willing to assume the responsibility for growth is that *they were not prepared for such a role in seminary*. In fact much seminary training, particularly through the 1960s and 1970s and even some today, has stressed exactly the opposite. Pastors are taught to be enablers rather than leaders. A revived emphasis on the laypeople of the church as members of the Body of Christ has caused the pendulum to swing too far in the other direction. The pastor is taught to function as a member of the Body and not as a leader of the Body. Ted Engstrom says, "All strong leaders become so because they are able to identify readily with people but not become 'one of the boys.' A leader has to be ready to walk away from the crowd and be alone."[5] This has not been stressed in recent ministerial training. In the next chapter I am going to discuss it in much more detail and suggest alternatives to the enabler model for the pastor.

Because seminary training has been deficient in this area, many practicing pastors do not know how to assume leadership in their congregations even if they want to. Fortunately, more courses in leadership development and organizational management are being introduced in seminary curricula, and continuing education opportunities for such studies are increasingly available.[6] I recommend that pastors who intend to lead their churches in growth take advantage of such offerings.

A third reason why some pastors are not willing to assume responsibility for growth is that *they are not sure of God's call*. This is a formidable drawback to a person dedicated to the service of God. If a pastor is not sure that he or she is in exactly the church of God's choice, motivation to pay the price for growth is very low. John Wimber recently researched churches of over 200 members growing at 100 percent per decade or more. Among his findings: "First, the pastors knew God had called them to the ministry. Second, we found they knew they were called to their place of ministry."[7] Church growth pastors harbor very little doubt that God has placed them in their particular church and that they will be there for a long time. They are not looking for greener pastures.

Not only are they sure that God has called them to a particular church, but they are sure that God has called them to be its leader. One of the most rapidly growing churches in Southern California is the Saddleback Valley Community Church, a Southern Baptist Church in Laguna Hills. Their pastor, Rick Warren, is a church growth pastor. They celebrated their third anniversary on Easter Sunday, 1983, with 1,000 in attendance. His announced growth goal is 20,000 members by the year 2020 plus starting a new church every year. So far they have started three new churches in three years. One of Warren's qualities is an assurance of his call. I am impressed with his letterhead. Across the top in bold letters are the words "Richard Warren, Pastor." The church name is in small type along the bottom of the page. I showed this letterhead to another pastor friend of mine who exclaimed, "This goes against the grain of all I ever learned in seminary!" He said that he was taught the institution was what counted most and that the church should have been featured on the stationery with the pastor's name in small print. It offended his sense of pastoral modesty.

It is easy to comprehend my friend's feeling. Ultimately, the Body of Christ is the most important, and this is understood by those who are biblical Christians and serving the Lord. But Warren's letterhead is not designed to impress Christians, it is targeted toward non-Christians, the 20,000 of them he hopes to win to Christ over the next thirty or forty years. An interesting survey was recently done in Georgia. It asked unchurched people what would be the one thing that would most encourage them to select a particular

church. The highest factor by far was the pastor.
The pastor was substantially more important to
those unbelievers than the denomination, the
facilities, the friendliness, the church program,
the doctrine, and even whether they have friends
who go there. Rick Warren knows this and he also
knows that God has called him to build a great
church. He himself is a modest person, but he is
also willing to assume the responsibility for the
growth of his church.

Working hard

The second price that pastors must pay if they
are going to lead their church into growth is hard
work. Let's face it. It is not an easy job to lead a
growing church. Some months ago, as I was fin-
ishing a two-week seminar, one of the pastors put
up his hand and said, "I can summarize these two
weeks in two words: hard work!" And I have no
intention to surgarcoat the pill. The church
growth pastors I know are putting in long hours in
planning, meeting with people who influence the
growth process in one way or another, in prayer
and the seeking of God's leading, in study and
research, in putting out fires, but most of all in
dreaming God's dreams after Him. And all this on
top of the routine duties of being a pastor.

Worldwide one of the flash points of church
growth is Korea. One hundred years ago there
were no Christians in Korea. Now Christians
make up almost 30 percent of the population and
should be over 50 percent by the end of 1980s.
There are many factors entering into Korean
church growth, but one is the assumption that
the pastor is the leader of the church. Korean pastors have a great deal of authority. They are loved
and respected. They are well taken care of. Korean

mothers pray that their daughters will marry a pastor just as mothers in other countries pray that they will marry a doctor or a lawyer. But Korean pastors work hard for their money. Every Korean pastor is up long before daybreak seven days a week, leading the dawn prayer meeting in the church at 4:30 or 5:00 A.M. On most days they work far into the evening as well. I admire them greatly.

The nature of the pastorate invites laziness. Accountability for occupational hours is low. Pastors do not punch a time clock. The job is done at many locations: the church, the pastor's home, the automobile, the hospital, the homes of church members, and enough other places that no one can keep track of where the pastor is at any given time. Few other wage-earning Americans enjoy the degree of freedom that characterizes the ministry. But the freedom carries with it a responsibility, and if a pastor does not have the self-discipline to carry it well, improvement in that area should be an item high on their prayer list.

I am not advocating workaholism. I am not suggesting that a pastor should put the work ahead of the family. I am looking for a balance between intensive work, creative leisure, and quality time with loved ones. Still I am describing a church growth pastor. Lee Lebsack, who saw his Assemblies of God church in Ravenna, Ohio, grow from 200 to 2,000 in six years, studied ten of the largest churches in the Assemblies of God. One thing he found is that the pastors of all ten churches were great leaders. And then he says, "A common denominator of all these pastors . . . is their strong work habits. They are not lazy men, but work hard. Their churches reflect their efforts."[8]

While pastoring a growing church is hard work, it is also enjoyable. One of my closest friends is John Wimber, pastor of Vineyard Christian Fellowship of Yorba Linda, California. I remember a little over six years ago when he started with seventeen in his living room. They are now meeting in a high school gymnasium, serving about 5,000 people. I like the way Wimber describes his feelings: "I love my job. I like to get up in the morning and do what I did yesterday. It's fun to be in a growing church. We baptized 337 people last year. That's fun; that's exciting!"[9]

For many pastors, part of the hard work involved in becoming a church growth pastor is to learn how churches grow. Back in the days when most of us went to seminary and Bible school there were no courses in church growth, no professors of church growth, no books on church growth. While evangelism was taught, most of the emphasis was on maintaining the given institution and taking care of the needs of the church members. John Wimber, for example, did not become a church growth pastor by accident. During the first years of his pastoral ministry back in the early 1970s, he made a simple observation: there were ten churches in his immediate area with over 2,000 members each. Obviously, these pastors were doing something that John wasn't doing. So he set out to establish a personal relationship with as many of them as he could. Within a year, he was meeting regularly with four of them, soaking up what they knew. One result of that effort is that now, ten years later, hundreds of pastors are seeking out John Wimber to discuss what he is doing right.

My point is that all this took time, energy, and effort. It was hard work to make contact with those four pastors, but the work paid off. Those who need to supplement their seminary training now have many opportunities for learning about church growth available to them, but all require work. If you are willing to pay the price, here are several suggestions:

Visit and study growing churches. Feeling is an important dimension of leading a church to growth. When you think of it, most American pastors have never really felt growth. They were raised in a church that was not growing, at seminary they interned in one or more non-growing churches, their first pastorates were in small non-growing churches and their present church is not growing either. If this describes your case, you need to get the growth feeling, and one of the best ways is to go there. You can go on your own, or you can attend a seminar that some growing church pastors put on. As a longtime member of the faculty of the Robert H. Schuller Institute for Successful Church Leadership, I myself have observed significant attitudinal changes in the pastors and lay church leaders who have come to the Crystal Cathedral over the years. Just a few days in a growing church can make a tremendous difference.

Read church growth books. The literature in the field of church growth has increased rapidly over the past ten years or so. Some excellent materials are available. I suggest that you set as a goal reading one new church growth book per month. You can order your own or join the American Church Growth Book Club which I established some years ago when I found that the average Christian book store does not concentrate on keeping up its inventory of church growth books. The book club informs you of twelve selections per year and you can order the ones you want. [10]

Attend church growth seminars and work-shops. The Institute of American Church Growth, directed by Win Arn, has been the leader through the years in conducting seminars and workshops on different aspects of church growth. Many other fine organizations are now doing it as well. Denominational bodies are holding them for their own clergy and lay leaders. I mentioned previously that some growing local churches conduct them from time to time. My good friend Larry Dewitt, pastor of the Calvary Community of Thousand Oaks, California, has had so much demand on his time from other pastors that he now sets aside one day per month for receiving pastors and other church leaders and sharing with them what the Lord has been teaching him. Gestures like this provide wonderful opportunities to learn more about church growth.

Take courses in church growth. Check with nearby seminaries and Bible schools for offerings in church growth available to pastors for continu-ing education. Through the years I think I have been of most help to American pastors through my teaching in the Fuller Doctor of Ministry program. This is the only program I am aware of which has a strong specialization in church growth for the D. Min. Of the required 40 units (plus dissertation or supervised ministry project), up to 28 units can be taken directly in church growth. The schedule is arranged so that you can pick up 12 of those units in any one of the two-week residence periods (hav-ing done substantial reading beforehand and writ-ing papers afterward). The doctoral level courses can be taken both by those who are enrolled in the program and by those who wish them simply for continuing education. The seminary accepts about 140 persons per year into the church growth courses.[11]

Sharing the ministry

A third price that pastors must pay if they expect their church to grow is to share their ministry. This must be done with other program staff as well as with laity.

It is not altogether accurate to say that growth cannot take place well if a pastor does not share the ministry. One person can handle pretty well all of the ministry of a small church. A pastor can do all the preaching, the teaching, the administration, the counseling, the committee meetings, the fund raising, the mission program, the community relations, the visitation, and the outreach activities almost singlehandedly. But for the average pastor the energy for continuing to do all the ministry runs out when the church reaches the 200 plateau. Churches can grow up to the 200 barrier without shared ministry, but they cannot go much further than that.

Before developing the theme of sharing the ministry any further I should say a few words about the notorious 200 barrier. The years of research I have done into the growth dynamics of churches has uncovered the figure of 200 as a numerical ceiling on growth. I am aware that other researchers have suggested different figures for leveling off. David A. Womack, for example, has one of the longer lists with 35, 85, 125, 180, 240, 280, 400, 600, 800 and 1200 as critical points.[12] I have no reason to doubt that these are significant growth points except that in actual field diagnosis I have not found any of them consistently a problem. The 200 barrier is different. It has turned up time and again. It is no accident that a full 80 percent of American churches are at 200 or under. Lyle Schaller calls it the "awkward size," and I agree. Leadership decisions made at the 200 barrier have more influence on the future of a given congregation than those at any other point.

I am necessarily generalizing. The 200 figure implies a range. It has no magic in itself. What I mean by the phrase *200 barrier*, which I will use a great deal in this book, is a range of something between 150 and 250 active members. Active members are those whose names belong on the church roll. They may not be there every Sunday, but they attend at least occasionally, they make some financial contribution to the church, they regard the church as "my church," they expect that their young children will also become members, and they look to the church for rites of passage such as weddings and funerals. In other words they expect that the church and its personnel will minister to them in a somewhat regular way. *Numerically* speaking (keeping in mind that other drastic things can also enter the picture) when a given local church has between 150 and 250 people whose participation is at least at the level I have just described it will run into its most serious growth problems. Churches under the 200 barrier have a certain predictable set of characteristics, and churches over the 200 barrier have a different set.

I will mention several of those as we go on, but at this point we are dealing with sharing the ministry. If the church is to break the 200 barrier, the pastor must begin sharing the ministry. It is not good to wait until growth stops at around 200 and then decide to start sharing ministry. It should be done as far back as possible in order to avoid losing growth momentum. It is much more difficult to pick up after a loss of momentum than to prevent it.

At a later point I am going to discuss in some detail how to staff a church for growth. Suffice it to say here that before the church slows down at the 200 barrier at least one more program staff person should be on board. Adding a staff member, however, is too much of a price for some pastors to pay. They are so constituted that they are loners. They will never be happy either as a member of someone else's staff or in charge of a staff of their own. This is not a reprehensible personality trait, but it is a restriction on growth.

Sharing the ministry with laity is another question, but just as difficult for some. Some pastors feel that laypeople aren't qualified for ministry because they have had no professional training in seminary or Bible school. Some are threatened by the possibility that a layperson could minister in some area even better than they could. Some feel an obligation to earn their salary by doing all the ministry themselves and unfortunately some have strong church members who reinforce this by saying, "Well, what are we paying you for anyway?" Whatever the reason, not being able to share ministry with laypeople is a serious obstacle to church growth.

Sharing the ministry is called "delegation" by management experts. I recently read in one of Ted Engstrom's books about five reasons why leaders fail to delegate. These five apply to sharing ministry on both staff and lay levels and bear mentioning:

1. They believe the subordinates won't be able to handle the assignment.
2. They fear competition from subordinates.
3. They are afraid of losing recognition.

4. They are fearful their weaknesses will be exposed.

5. They feel they won't have the time to turn over the work and provide the necessary training.[13]

In counseling with scores of pastors, I have heard each one of these problems mentioned time and again. It is not hard to see why sharing the ministry is simply too high a price for some pastors to pay for growth.

Having members you can't pastor

This sounds strange at first. How can a pastor have members that he or she cannot pastor?

First let me explain what I mean by pastoring in this context. Most of the time in this book I am using the term *pastor* to refer to the chief executive officer of a local church, often referred to as the senior pastor or the minister. In this context, however, I am using the term *pastor* in a more literal sense. I am referring to the one-on-one relationship that a pastor has with each parishioner. It is a very traditional model of a pastor, expected by many congregations of the person they hire. If you have the heart of a pastor or a shepherd you have a need to know the names of all your church members and their families, visit each home x number of times per year, make an extra call or two to everyone who is sick, do all the counseling, perform all the baptisms, weddings and funerals, lend a hand in personal problems, and enjoy a type of family relationship with one and all.

This can be done up to the 200 barrier. In some rare cases it can even be stretched a little more. But in order to get through the 200 barrier and sustain a healthy rate of growth, the pastor must be willing to pay a price too high for some: he or she must be willing to shift from a *shepherd* mode to a *rancher* mode.

I am indebted to Lyle E. Schaller for this graphic terminology, and he traces it to an off-hand comment by a Presbyterian minister in Texas.[14] It fits the bill perfectly. Notice that in a church led by a rancher the sheep are still shepherded, but the rancher does not do it. The rancher sees that it is done by others.

It is not easy for an American pastor to be anything other than a shepherd. A vast majority not only are shepherds, but their congregations demand that they remain that way. Schaller observes that "the shepherd role is probably the appropriate ministerial style for the pastor of those congregations averaging less than one hundred and fifty at the principal weekly worship service . . . but that pastoral role tends to inhibit the evangelistic outreach of those congregations."[15] In other words, it is an obstacle to growth.

On the weekend between the two weeks of class in my Doctor of Ministry Church Growth I course here at Fuller, the pastors visit churches out in the field and interview both the staff and some laypeople. One question they ask the laypeople is, "Why do you stay in this church?" One of the churches they research is the Crystal Cathedral, a church of 10,000 members. Amazingly enough, a consistent answer from laypeople in the Crystal Cathedral is, "This is the friendliest church in Orange County!" How can this be?

A major reason why this happens is that the pastor, Robert H. Schuller, is a rancher par excellence. He has a great heart for his people, but he is realistic enough to know that he cannot shepherd them one-on-one. Most members of the Crystal Cathedral feel they have had close contact with their pastor if they get to shake hands with Schuller every six months or so. But Schuller has taken pains, through delegation to an associate named David Bailey, for the training of an elite group of 700 "lay ministers of pastoral care." These gifted men and women have each had up to 250 classroom hours of academic training in ministry provided by the church itself. They are trained in Bible, theology, counseling, church history, pastoral work, and most of the areas they would study if they went to seminary. They are officially commissioned as ministers by the congregation. Each of them is assigned to ten to fifteen families of the church for whom they are responsible. They, not Pastor Schuller, are the shepherds. When one of their group is sick or has a problem, they are on hand. If they run into a situation they cannot handle, they then refer it to the church staff. They visit the homes and the hospitals. An average member of the Crystal Cathedral is contacted once a month by a minister of the church, sometimes by telephone, sometimes by visit, sometimes through the mail. No wonder they consider it the friendliest church in Orange County! Many people in a small country church do not have that much personal attention from a minister.

The first time I met Charles Allen, pastor of First Methodist Church, Houston, Texas, I got a surprise. Naturally I was interested in how he managed to lead a church of 12,000 members—at that time the largest Methodist church in the world. "Well," he said, "for one thing I visit every family once a quarter." When he saw that my mouth fell open, a twinkle came to his eye. "Do you think God will let liars into heaven?" he asked. That was his vivid way of letting me know he was a rancher.

Revising non-growth theology

A fifth and final price that some pastors must pay for moving their church into growth is to rethink and revise some of their theology. This is impossible for some who have a strong ego identification with certain theological positions, especially if those positions have been reinforced by publication. In the last chapter I mentioned liberal theology and the role I believe it has had in membership decline in the mainline churches. There is no need to elaborate on that further here except to report that I think there is some movement away from liberal theology to a more biblical and evangelical theology among practicing mainline pastors. I would hesitate to call it a trend, but on several occasions in recent years I have been conversing with pastors who have said, somewhat casually, "When I used to be a liberal . . . " Of course the ones who have made such a theological switch would be those most likely to show up in one of my church growth courses or seminars.

I will limit my comments here to two theological positions that cut across the liberal-evangelical spectrum, but that have proven to be theological obstacles to growth.

Remnant theology. Years ago Donald McGavran coined the term *remnant theology* and it has since become part of standard church growth jargon. It has arisen, he says, in areas where Christian work has suffered not only slow growth but decades of defeat. He describes it as "a glorification of littleness . . . in which to be small is to be holy. Slow growth is adjudged good growth."[16] Gideon and his army constitute a paradigm for remnant theologians. Books are published with titles such as *Small Churches Are Beautiful, Small Churches Are the Right Size,* and as has been mentioned, *Church Growth Is Not the Point.* Remnant theologians are highly suspicious of churches with large memberships and elevated decadal growth rates.

Faithfulness vs. success. A frequent statement by those defending non-growth is, "God has called us to be faithful, not successful." 1 Corinthians 4:2 is often used to back this up: "Moreover it is required in stewards that one be found faithful." I have never been able to comprehend setting faithfulness over against stewardship, however. It seems to me that biblically they go together. One of Jesus' central teachings on stewardship is His parable of the talents. In it He describes a scene from the commercial world where the master gives three servants $1,000, $2,000 and $5,000 respectively (to substitute modern currency figures). The goal for each is to make more money. The one with $2,000 brings back $4,000 and the one with $5,000 brings back $10,000. What does the master say to each? "Well done, good and *faithful* servant." They were faithful because they were successful in taking the master's resources and using them for the master's purpose. The unfaithful servant did not accomplish the master's goal, or in other words he was unsuccessful.

Since the theological position of setting faithfulness against success sounded so modest and so pious, it was usually not recognized as a non-growth point of view. But more recently it is being questioned in the mainline denominations where it has mostly been used. In the United Presbyterian Task Force on Church Membership report, for example, Edward Brubaker says, "We need to stop justifying, to stop blaming the wrong causes, to stop wringing our hands and instead clearly affirm that church growth is a natural result of faithfulness and obedience to the Gospel."[17] I agree with Brubaker that it is high time to recognize that if we are faithful to God in our Christian life and witness, churches generally speaking will grow. There are, of course, exceptions to the rule, but they clearly are exceptions. When growth conditions are favorable, rationalizations based on theology should not be used as excuses for nongrowth.

The People's Price for Growth

We have seen five prices that pastors must pay for growth. Now it is time to look into four prices that the people in the congregation must pay if they expect their church to grow.

Agreeing to follow growth leadership

If a strong pastoral leadership role is as important as I think it is, a strong followership role for the people is equally important. The litmus test for a leader is that there be followers, and that those followers be voluntary. I have talked to many a frustrated pastor who wants to lead the church to growth but cannot because the people in the church refuse to grant permission.

The analogy of the pastor and the sheep, taken from the agricultural world, is a powerful analogy. If I had made it up as a literary device I would be suspicious of it because it is so strong. My background is agriculture and my college degree is animal husbandry. While I haven't been a sheep farmer, I know enough about sheep to know that they are the most dependent and vulnerable animals on the farm. Cows and pigs and horses and goats and dogs are all more intelligent and self-sufficient than sheep. The role the pastor has in the life of the sheep is awesome. But I did not invent this analogy, it is a biblical analogy. Church leaders are called pastors in the Bible and the people are called the flock.

Agreeing to be sheep and being willing to follow the growth leadership of a pastor is a price too high for the people of some congregations to pay for growth. If attitudes do not change, the growth potential for their church remains low. It is such an important matter that I will enlarge on it in a future chapter, so nothing further needs to be said at this point.

Paying the money

Church growth costs money. Yes, there are some experimental church growth projects which are more economical than the average, but by and large it will continue to cost money. Obviously this money must ultimately come from the church members.

As I have observed growing churches I find an excitement in the air, a kind of electricity. The people believe in what is happening, and they are willing to pay the bills. Stingy, miserly, penny-pinching congregations are not typically growth congregations. Members of growth congregations are cheerful givers, and God loves them as He said He would.

I have found that giving generously for growth is not usually a starting point. It is not a cause, it is an effect. It is clearly associated with the first price for a congregation, that of agreeing to follow growth leadership. If the proper dynamic of pastor-people relationship develops, people are much more inclined to listen to reason about their giving. They need a cause they really believe in if they are going to be motivated to support it.

This is just an introduction. I will elaborate on

it later, along with the need to develop congregational followership.

Readjusting their fellowship groups

One of the greatest blessings of being a Christian is to enjoy Christian fellowship. Churches which do not provide meaningful opportunities for Christian brothers and sisters to fellowship with one another are usually not growing churches. Because interpersonal relationships are such a high priority to most Christians, it is easy to see why disturbing them would be too high a price for some people to pay for growth.

At its worst, the desire to preserve accustomed patterns of Christian fellowship can actually repel strangers. I look at this as a disease and call it "koinonitis," derived from the biblical word for fellowship, *koinonia*. It is koinonia gone bad, fellowship inflammation. Christian people get enjoying each other's company so much that they lose the vision for reaching the unchurched people around them. Strangers become a threat, so they are effectively excluded from the fellowship circles. Growth is not only a low priority, it is something to be avoided.

I cannot think of any churches in which I have heard the above feelings verbalized. Everyone knows it is not a Christian attitude. Most Christians affirm their desire to reach out and share the good news with others. As a matter of fact, many people from churches which have acute koinonitis will read this and say, "I'm glad he's not describing us!" That is because in many cases the attitude is entirely subconscious. But while the people in the church may not be able to recognize that they have koinonitis, the newcomers do, and in a very short period of time. They can feel the gap between the smile and the handshake at the church door and the impenetrable social barrier around the fellowship groups.

This is an obstacle to growth in both small churches and large churches. In small churches it relates to the 200 barrier that was mentioned previously. I pointed out that in order to get through the 200 barrier, pastors must be willing (a) to share their ministry and (b) to have members that they cannot pastor one-on-one. Now here is where some responsibility for breaking the 200 barrier falls squarely on the shoulders of the laypeople. They must be willing to readjust their fellowship patterns.

The small church, as has been pointed out previously, is a single-cell church. And a single-cell has some distinct values. It has an integrity all its own. Single-cell churches are good churches. But if they decide that they will remain a single cell they cannot grow. The reason for this is a rather simple sociological principle. The human being has the capacity to relate to a fairly limited number of other persons on a face-to-face basis. The suggested numbers for this vary from study to study, but when any such group passes 100, the strain involved in trying to attach names to faces is evident, particularly for those who attend worship services every week but who do not participate in other church activities to any significant extent. That is why, when the group gets up to 150 or 200, its capacity to absorb new members has been taxed to the utmost. Either changes have to be made or the church will stop growing.

What are the changes? Forming new options for adult fellowship groups. This is not easy for most people because it means leaving some old friends and making some new ones.

In larger churches which already have multiple options for adult fellowship groups, koinonitis can also halt growth. The existing groups get either too large or too exclusivistic so that new members cannot locate entry points. Many of these new members, frustrated by what they perceive to be social rejection, will go out the back door and turn up in some other church where they can find fellowship. In large churches new fellowship groups should continually be started, but it requires constant effort to make sure it happens. The pastor needs to give leadership to the process, but if the people are unwilling to pay the price the chances are it will not happen and the church will not grow.

Opening their leadership circles

In some churches, not all, a relatively small group of laypeople have gained leadership control of the church and they have decided they will retain it. They feel a sense of personal ownership, and they have developed effective mechanisms of self-protection. They protect their leadership circle on two sides: against new laypeople and against pastors.

As long as the church is not growing, the leaders do not have to be much concerned about new laypeople taking over leadership. The social pecking order of the existing congregation is in most cases cordially agreed upon by the active members of the church, and the status quo will ordinarily be maintained without much effort. Oh, changes can take place in the formal structures. A different board member here, and a different chairperson there. But functionally, everybody knows who really runs the church. Often the real power center of a church might not be on the official board at all. It might be the wife of an elder or a man who had "retired" from the board of trustees several years back but who still is the heaviest donor to the church. The functional leadership structure is never spoken of in public or written down in reports.

However, when a church begins to grow and new people begin coming into the church, a different social situation emerges. A predictable conflict is on the horizon. This has been called by Lyle Schaller the "pioneer-homesteader conflict" and, at least in my experience, is easily the most pervasive and most devastating conflict problem facing the clergy today. Failure to understand the pioneer-homesteader conflict has meant failure to probably thousands of practicing pastors. Most have either resigned from the congregation or capitulated to the pioneers, but in either case it has been a serious obstacle to growth.

A Christian and Missionary Alliance pastor from Pennsylvania was one of scores who have told me their pioneer-homesteader story. His is one of the few that has a happy ending. It seems that the pioneers of the church would not accept his leadership for a long time. So he decided to make a strategic move. It would be hard to guess what he did. He locked the organ! The organist was a pioneer. This brought the power crisis to a head and the struggle lasted for six months. During that time the congregation sang with piano only. Then the pioneers repented, pledged their loyalty to the pastor, and he promptly unlocked the organ. Harmony was restored, and the church began to grow. Most of the time, however, it is not that easy. I will have more to say about pioneers and homesteaders in a later chapter.

The second side the entrenched lay leaders protect themselves on is against pastors. They intuitively resist allowing a pastor to assume the functional leadership of the church, and they have devised a foolproof way of keeping this from happening. They simply change their pastor every two, three, or four years.

Lyle E. Schaller says "there is overwhelmingly persuasive evidence that from a *long-term congregational* perspective, the most productive years of a pastorate seldom *begin* before the fourth or fifth or sixth year of a minister's tenure in that congregation."[18] This means if they can get rid of the pastor soon enough, the pastor's productive years in that church will never begin.

Study after study has reinforced the positive correlation between ministerial longevity and church growth. Beasley-Murray and Wilkinson's survey in England found that "it is not until a minister has served for 5 to 10 years in his church that a bias towards growth becomes apparent." Beasley-Murray himself admits that "this finding has significantly altered my own approach to the ministry at Altrincham. Initially I had seen myself as ministering for a relatively short period of time, particularly as it is my first pastorate."[19] No wonder that the Altrincham Baptist Church is now growing at over 200 percent per decade.

It needs to be recognized that the pattern of short-term pastorates is something relatively new. In the early days of our nation, a pastor would assume that a call to a church was a lifetime situation. The same with a doctor or a lawyer. Of the 550 Yale graduates who entered the Congregational ministry between 1702 and 1794, seven out of ten spent their entire ministerial career with the first church they served.[20] In many denominations this pattern prevailed into our own century.

But times have changed and, at least in white American churches, tenure has become much shorter. In black churches it hasn't changed, and it is not unusual to find black pastors who have led their congregations for thirty or forty years. The only exceptions are black pastors in predominantly white denominations such as the United Methodists. Massey and McKinney call this "the sweet fruits of a long pastorate."[21] A prominent feature in the annual church calendar in black churches is the celebration of the minister's anniversary as pastor.

All the blame for high pastoral mobility cannot be placed on the lay leaders of the congregation. As William Willimon says, "We should be honest about our highly mobile clergy: clerical moving is most often motivated by a concern for the career and salary advancement of the individual clergypersons; rarely out of a concern for the congregations."[22] Pastors need to recognize the fact that there are two ways to get a larger church. Either move to another one or stay where you are and lead the present church to growth. With the proper relationships between pastor and laypeople, and a willingness on the part of both to pay the price for growth, the latter can happen much more frequently than it has.

Notes

1. Elmer L. Towns, John N. Vaughan and David J. Seifert, *The Complete Book of Church Growth* (Wheaton: Tyndale House Publishers, 1981). Vaughan wrote the chapter on "The Fuller Factor." See p. 109.

2. Larry Richards, *InterCHANGE* newsletter, Step 2, Chicago, Illinois, vol. 1, no. 5.

3. C. Edward Brubaker, "Program for Increasing Membership," *The Presbyterian Layman*, June/July 1976, p. 5.

4. D. Dewayne Davenport, *The Bible Says Grow: Church Growth Guidelines for Church of Christ* (Williamstown, WV: Evangelism Seminar, 1978), p. 30.

5. Ted W. Engstrom, *The Making of a Christian Leader* (Grand Rapids: Zondervan Publishing House, 1976), p. 97.

6. Fuller Seminary's Institute for Christian Organizational Development offers regular courses in leadership, and many of them are open to pastors for continuing education. Write 135 N. Oakland Avenue, Pasadena, CA 91101.

7. John Wimber, "The Church Growth Pastor," *Higher Goals*, Gwen Jones, ed. (Springfield, MO: Gospel Publishing House, 1978), p. 48.

8. Lee Lebsack, *Ten at the Top: How Ten of America's Largest Assemblies of God Churches Grew* (Grand Rapids: Baker Book House, 1974), p. 115.

9. Wimber, "The Church Growth Pastor," p. 52.

10. For information on the American Church Growth Book Club write P.O. Box 90095, Pasadena, CA 91109-5095.

11. For more information about Doctor of Ministry level courses in church growth write Fuller Theological Seminary, 135 N. Oakland Avenue, Pasadena, CA 91101.

12. David A. Womack, *The Pyramid Principle of Church Growth* (Minneapolis: Bethany Fellowship, 1977), p. 17.

13. Engstrom, *The Making of a Christian Leader*, p. 164.

14. Lyle E. Schaller, *Survival Tactics in the Parish* (Nashville: Abingdon Press, 1977), p. 53.

15. *Ibid.*, p. 54.

16. Donald A. McGavran, *Understanding Church Growth* (Grand Rapids: Wm. B. Eerdmans Publishing Co., 1980 and in Britain by S.P.C.K.), p. 168.

17. C. Edward Brubaker, "Program for Increasing Membership," p. 5.

18. Lyle E. Schaller, *Assimilating New Members* (Nashville: Abingdon Press, 1978), p. 53.

19. Paul Beasley-Murray and Alan Wilkinson, *Turning the Tide: An Assessment of Baptist Church Growth in England* (London: Bible Society, 1981), p. 34.

20. Lyle E. Schaller, "When Should the Pastor Move?" *The Christian Ministry*, July, 1980, p. 26.

21. Floyd Massey, Jr. and Samuel Berry McKinney, *Church Administration in the Black Perspective* (Valley Forge: Judson Press, 1976), p. 27.

22. William H. Willimon, "Unifying Factors for a Congregation," unpublished paper, p. 46.

3

Church Growth Pastor = Leader + Equipper

The principal argument of this book is that if churches are going to maximize their growth potential they need pastors who are strong leaders. The point requires thorough explanation because it is not commonly expressed. There may be exceptions, as there are to any church growth principle, but make no mistake about it: it is a rule. If your church is not growing and you wonder why, take a close look at the roles of the pastor. In some cases you won't have to look much further to discover your major barrier to growth.

The Decline of the "Enabler" Ideal

One reason why strong pastoral leadership is not characteristic of many of America's churches is that in the recent past clergy have been taught just the opposite in the seminaries. Many pastors learned from their seminary professors that they should not abuse their leadership positions in the churches. They were taught to reject strong, authoritative, directive pastoral leadership. A whole vocabulary has been developed to discredit pastors who have tended toward aggressive leadership. It is called "dictatorial," conjuring up images of Hitler or Idi Amin. It is said to be "Jim Jones" type of leadership, so obnoxious to sensitive Christians. Some put it this way: "Christianity needs no ayatollahs!" Pastors are warned against "ego trips" and "empire building."

The alternative has been the model of the pastor as an "enabler." Many practicing pastors tend to measure their role in the church against the characteristics of the enabler. This is true particularly of clergy now in the thirty to forty-five age bracket, but others do so as well.

The enabler model arose and became popular in the seminaries for a good reason. Pastoral leadership in many American churches had become "clericalism." The clergy were the active components of the church system while the laypeople were passive components. The enabler idea was originally intended to stress two things: first, the servant role of pastors and second, the need for them to equip the laity for ministry. I agree that both of these are essential for effective church growth leadership, but the model went awry as I will explain.

While I knew for a long time that there was something wrong with the enabler model, I could not quite put my finger on what it was. It took two of my favorite contemporary authors to shed the light I needed. They were Presbyterian Richard G. Hutcheson in his book *The Wheel Within the Wheel* and Methodist Lyle E. Schaller in his *Effective Church Planning*, both published in 1979. When I read these books I began to understand why, good as the motivation behind the enabler ideal was, it had not helped churches to grow, generally speaking.

What, exactly, is an enabler?

Richard Hutcheson puts it this way: "An enabler or facilitator is a relatively uninvolved technician who understands the process by which things are accomplished and who enables others to achieve goals."[1] Lyle Schaller, with his characteristic literary technique of staging a fictitious dialogue to serve as a case study, has a layperson describe a former pastor. "We called a self-identified enabler type minister," he said, "and we got burned. We found the word enabler was a synonym for not being an initiator, not calling, not being aggressive, and not taking leadership responsibilities."[2]

Where Did the "Enabler" Come From?

The idea of the pastor as an enabler reflects some general trends in American society over the past few decades. World War II created a strong sentiment against dictators. It vividly portrayed how leadership authority could be abused. It is understandable how an anti-authority strain could creep into American social psychology.

Hutcheson traces it back to the human relations movement of the 1940s associated with Kurt Lewin and group dynamics theory. The major values of the movement stressed interpersonal relationships. Planning and control within an organization were frowned upon. Decisions were to be made through collegiality, mutuality, and group activity, but not through the exercise of authority which Hutcheson says is "perhaps the dirtiest word in its lexicon."[3]

These social values had their impact on the radical theologies of the 1960s and the popularity of sensitivity and encounter groups, individual self-fulfillment, and the supreme emphasis on people, not organizations. Seminaries picked this up and taught nondirective counseling techniques, relational theology, and the enabler model for the pastor. The pastor's major task was not to move the organization (the church) ahead or to be concerned with its growth. Helping the church members rise through Maslow's hierarchy of needs and become self-actualized persons was the goal. Someone said that if you asked a pastor with this training what time of the day it was, you would get one of two answers: "Why do you ask?" or "What time would you like it to be?"

By the late 1960s not only had seminary students been taught this pastoral ideal, but many practicing ministers had been retooled with the concept. A large number of American churches, particularly those whose pastors were college graduates, were experimenting with the enabler type of leader. It may or may not have been coincidental that the mainline churches began their epochal membership decline just at that time; but for one thing, the enabler leadership model was not what the churches needed to turn the trends around. Of course it was not fashionable even to want them turned around. In fact many church leaders were saying that the loss of members was a good thing. They were so anti-institutional that some were preaching that the church should die like a grain of wheat falling into the ground and then we would see what God could bring out of the ruins! Growth of the "institutional church" was considered an almost disreputable objective for ministry.

As Lyle Schaller sees it, "While it is impossible to affix precise dates on trends such as this one, it appears that the concept of the pastor as an enabler peaked in popularity in the late 1960s and has been declining ever since."[4]

The net results of the prominence of the enabler model over two or three decades is both good and bad. The good news is that it did away with clericalism for the most part. There is now a new and valuable stress on the role of the laity in the life of the church. The priesthood of all believers is reaffirmed and practiced widely. The wave of emphasis on body life and spiritual gifts that is bringing so much life and renewal to the churches is one of its positive outcomes.

But while this emphasis has been and will continue to be healthy, the bad news side of the enabler model has been sufficiently strong to hinder church growth, particularly in the mainline denominations. With all the stress on the need for lay ministry, the pastor tended to forfeit his or her God-given leadership authority. Pastoral ministry has been people-oriented but not task-oriented. Key decisions were supposed to be made by groups, not individuals. Hutcheson concludes that "there is some evidence, indeed, that church organizations have been suffering from leaderlessness."[5] He even goes on to raise a fascinating theological issue when he asks "whether a persistent and long-term devaluation of authority in organizations may not subtly encourage a devaluation of authority relationship between God and humans."[6] If this is actually the case, it may further explain a relationship between the enabler model and mainline church decline.

The Pastor as Equipper

Observing that the enabler ideal probably peaked in the late 1960s does not mean that it has disappeared from the scene. Schaller says, "The concept still has wide support . . . and is still being advocated by many as the ideal role for a pastor by many professional (and professorial) preacher-watchers."[7] The mention of professorial types is Schaller's way of indicating that the enabler model is still taught in some seminaries. This, unfortunately, is the case. Few seminary textbooks, even today, argue strongly enough for authoritative pastoral leadership.

The enabler concept is proposed in books such as pastor Robert C. Girard's *Brethren, Hang Loose.* There he suggests that "In the years ahead the professional pastor's role must further diminish . . . . My vision calls for increasing dependence upon Spirit-filled men and women of our own who take over more and more of the ministry of the Word—the 'pulpit ministry.' " His plan is for the pastor to pull back and turn the whole church over to the laypeople.[8]

David Mains, founding pastor of the innovative Circle Church in Chicago, tells how he went through a significant transition in his own personal thinking. Circle Church was founded in the late 1960s, at the peak of the enabler concept. Ten years later Mains saw his dreams crumble. The first members of Circle were very much a part of the anti-authoritarian scene. The body life movement was just beginning. Mains now looks back and says, "In setting up the climate of leadership in the church, I stressed the equality of all believers to the exclusion of the hierarchical gifts of leadership. I discovered the fact too late; I couldn't turn the congregation around." He now sees that "if you push servant leadership too far you can turn the leader into a doormat and destroy him." And then he sounds a warning: "I believe this problem of minimizing the pastor's leadership is a disease spreading wildly through evangelical churches."[9]

The central challenge, as I see it, is to sustain the emphasis on freeing the laity of the church for significant ministry while at the same time restoring the role of the pastor as leader. This can be done, I believe, by describing the pastor as both leader and equipper. The equipper is different from the enabler. Here is my definition of an equipper:

An equipper is a leader who actively sets goals for a congregation according to the will of God, obtains goal ownership from the people, and sees that each church member is properly motivated and equipped to do his or her part in accomplishing the goals.

I put that statement in italics because I feel it is the central thrust of this book. If clergy can believe that their primary role is that of equipper and if the laypeople will give their consent and open the way for their pastor to be such a person, churches can grow both in quantity and in quality.

The larger the church gets, the more important it is that the pastor be an equipper. The enabler model will work to a degree in churches which have not yet reached the 200 barrier, but it cannot go much further. So if a church is going to crack the 200 barrier, it should look closely at the role of the pastor long before it gets there and possibly loses growth momentum. More about church size later.

What is the future of the enabler? While David Mains sees the idea spreading among evangelicals, indications are that at least among the mainline churches it now is being recognized as largely ineffective. Lyle Schaller, as we have seen, feels that it peaked in the late 1960s. If it did, it declined rather slowly during the first part of the 1970s. But by the end of the decade a significant research project conducted by Jackson W. Carroll and Robert L. Wilson revealed that in the current mainline job market, the pastor in most demand is "the one who provides strong leadership, makes things happen, is somewhat of an entrepreneur," while the candidate now being passed over is "the more passive person who waits for the people to take the lead."[10] In other words, the enabler is, or is becoming, passé.

Two Pastoral Dilemmas

Almost any pastor who tries to serve God in a biblical way is constantly faced with two classic dilemmas. Laypeople who want to know what makes their pastor tick need to understand these dilemmas very well, and their pastor probably won't tell them. It is something that the pastor cannot talk about readily. It must be acted out and felt. If verbalized, the laypeople are the ones who need to tell the pastor that he or she is doing well. It doesn't work the other way around.

The two dilemmas are: being both humble and powerful and being both a servant and a leader. Let's look at them one at a time.

Being both humble and powerful

Every biblical Christian is taught by Scripture not to be proud. Pride comes before a fall. "God resists the proud, but gives grace to the humble" (Jas. 4:6). No Christian is to "think of himself more highly than he ought to think" (Rom. 12:3). Humility is a Christian virtue consistently extolled in sermon and song. Pastors teach humility and try to model it in their daily lives.

But very few pastors adequately understand

the relationship that power has to humility. They seem like exact opposites, but in reality they are not. Jesus affirmed this as clearly as possible when He said, "Whoever exalts himself will be abased, and he who humbles himself will be exalted" (Matt. 23:12). Notice the two active verbs and the two passive verbs in this passage. The active verbs set forth our responsibility, while the passive verbs set forth God's response.

The first active verb is "exalts himself." It is humanly possible to take the initiative and exalt oneself. All too often a pastor will say words to the effect, "Now that I am your pastor, you *must* obey me." But true pastoral authority is not self-generating, it is bestowed by God. The pastor who tries to exalt himself or herself will find that God's response (the passive verb) causes them to "be abased." Self-exaltation is a way of committing the sin of pride.

The second active verb is "humbles himself." It is likewise possible for a person to take the initiative and decide to be humble. While we must acknowledge that humility is a fruit of the Spirit which comes ultimately through the grace of God, nevertheless being humble is something that we are commanded to do. James says straight out: "Humble yourselves in the sight of the Lord" (Jas. 4:10), and suggests that this activity take two forms. First we are to resist the devil (Jas. 4:7) and secondly we are to draw near to God (Jas. 4:8). Both of these relationships are loaded with meaning and should form the basis of regular spiritual self-inventories. But if we do actively humble ourselves, then we can expect to receive God's response (the passive verb). Jesus says that the humble person "will be exalted" and James says, "He will lift you up."

Many pastors with whom I have counseled have problems leading their church to growth because they accept the humility side of the dilemma, but not the power side. Jesus wants not one, but both. As a matter of fact, most of the strong pastors of growing churches I know are really humble persons, and they are recognized as such by those who know them well. Accusations of "ego trips" and the like are mostly made by relatively unattached outside observers who have some long-standing prejudices.

But it is easy to see why pastors themselves cannot affirm that they have arrived. They tell jokes about a make-believe book called *Humility and How I Attained It.* All this simply confirms that we are talking about a true dilemma, but one that needs to be faced realistically and courageously.

Being both a servant and a leader

The apostles James and John once tried to exalt themselves. They wanted to be Jesus' chief lieutenants in the kingdom. Jesus took the opportunity to teach all the apostles one of the most profound lessons about leadership. He first told them that, negatively, Christian leaders must not be like Gentiles and "lord it over them" (Mark 10:42). This contrast between lordship and leadership is again mentioned in 1 Peter 5, and I want to examine it in detail later on. But here Jesus goes on to the positive side and says, "Whoever desires to become great among you shall be your servant" (Mark 10:43). Christian leadership, in contrast to secular leadership, is based on servanthood. There is no other way to get it.

Notice that Jesus does not say that there is anything wrong with wanting to be a leader. However, He does say that in the Kingdom of God leadership does not come through coercion or self-imposition. It cannot be demanded, it must be earned. If the litmus test of a leader is that he or she has followers, those followers must perceive the person to be their servant before they will decide to follow.

But again here is where I find a problem in the ministry today. Many pastors will spend their lives proving that they are servants, but will not accept the consequence of doing that well, namely the exaltation that God gives them as a leader and the power that goes along with it. Jesus washed the disciples' feet, but at no time during His earthly ministry was there any doubt in His mind or the disciples' minds who their leader was. Servanthood and leadership do not contradict each other in Christian work. They go together.

Servanthood and Leadership Today

I think Dewayne Davenport sees the picture clearly. He suggests that it is humility itself which keeps many preachers from being true God-ordained leaders. A preacher will often deny that he or she is the key person for the growth of the church because "he fears what other preachers will think of him." He is also afraid of what the congregation will think. But Davenport's admonition is: "Preachers, it is your God-given responsibility to lead. Don't shrink from it."[11]

Leaders of growing churches today do not shrink from it. A while ago I visited the Kwang Lim Methodist Church in Seoul, Korea, pastored by my good friend Sundo Kim. Under his strong leadership, it has become the largest Methodist church in the world. Pastor Kim is perceived by his people, all 12,000 of them, to be their servant. Yet he, like most Korean pastors, has no problem with the dilemma between servanthood and leadership. The enabler model for the ministry has never been popular in Korea and that is one reason (among others) why their churches are growing so much faster than American churches. I was deeply impressed when Kim showed me the conference room in his church. There was a long table with seats for all the elders. At the head of the table were two chairs. Kim stood behind the chair on the right and said, "This is my chair. No human sits in the other—it is for Jesus Christ." The symbolism of Kim's affirming himself to be Jesus' right-hand person for the running of that local church seemed highly appropriate to me. Many American pastors, however, would have serious psychological and even theological problems with such an arrangement of furniture.

Another friend of mine, Jack Hayford, is the pastor of the nation's largest Foursquare Church, the Church on the Way in Van Nuys, California. Since he is my neighbor I have been able to watch the growth of that church fairly closely over the years. Some 5,000 people now attend the principal worship service every week. No one I know so ideally combines the roles of servant and leader. In a message to fellow pastors, Hayford recently said that "there is a desperate need for servants who will recognize their leadership role, commit themselves to it, and then get down off their pedestal and walk among the people . . . . People need to know that the leader has failed on occasion, but that, in his weakness he experienced the miraculous, surmounting power of God."[12] His starting point is servanthood.

But while Hayford consciously functions as a servant, he does not shy away from being exalted as a spokesperson for God in his congregation. He says that the laypeople he has built up in the faith and in their own leadership roles would never "attempt to usurp the place of the pastoral workers in the congregation," and that over the years "they loved and supported me on a level I had never before witnessed."[13] Once in a while Jack Hayford declares to his congregation, "God spoke to me and said . . . " I recall a few years ago, before the new sanctuary was completed, that in order to relieve the space problem he instructed his people that one Sunday morning per month instead of coming to the sanctuary they would meet with a house church group in their neighborhood. He said that he was announcing it as a part of the church's philosophy of ministry and that anyone who felt highly uncomfortable with it might better consider finding another church home. To emphasize his point, he said, "This is not Pastor Jack speaking to you. This is the Lord!"

I have told that story to numerous American pastors and have been fascinated by their reactions. Some are highly offended by a pastor who would assume so much authority in the local congregation. They think of it as arrogance. But Hayford explains. He says that he only uses the phrase "God spoke to me" on very special occasions. He does not mean that he learned something from revelation in general or that God gave him some private inner impression. What does he mean? He means that "at a given moment, almost always when I least expected it, the Lord spoke *words* to me. Those words have been so distinct that I am virtually able to say, 'And I quote . . . ' "[14] There is one reason above all that Jack Hayford is able to communicate with his people in that way: they perceive him to be their servant.

A third friend of mine, Gordon MacDonald, is pastor of the largest fast growing church in New England—Grace Chapel of Lexington, Massachusetts. They are currently running around 3,000 in Sunday worship. I know MacDonald well and salute him as one of America's outstanding evangelical leaders not only in his own congregation, but among his professional peers as well. This is why I was surprised when I read a recent article of his entitled, "Ten Conditions for Church Growth." What he said was excellent, but not one of the ten was strong pastoral leadership! So I wrote him and asked him why. In his reply he reminded me that he had frequently mentioned to me personally that no church he knew of could grow without strong pastoral leadership, and on the part of many pastors "this matter was subtly overlooked in the interest of a kind of pseudo-humility." Then he went on to confess that "here I am guilty of the same." He said if he were to rewrite the article he would put strong pastoral leadership up at the top. Incidentally, his letterhead, like Rick Warren's mentioned in an earlier chapter, has "Gordon MacDonald" across the top, and the name of the church down below. He, like the others, personifies not only authentic servanthood, but the leadership that needs to go along with it. [15]

The apostle Paul on many occasions referred to himself as a servant. Yet his authority was awesome. He saw no contradiction in being simultaneously a servant of Jesus Christ and an apostle (see Rom. 1:1). He did not hesitate to say to the Corinthians on two occasions, "Be followers of me" (see 1 Cor. 4:16; 11:1). On one of them he added, "as I am of Christ," acknowledging again his servanthood.

Larry Richards calls this a "strange contradiction." In researching three outstanding congregations he discovered that in all three "the leadership is strong and holds unusual authority in the church." But with all that, "the people never perceive their leaders as authoritarian . . . the people they serve enjoy submitting to them."[16] They have learned how to combine humility with power and servanthood with leadership.

Is a Manager a Leader?

The terms *manager* and *leader* are frequently used as synonyms. However, contemporary organizational theory suggests that there are some important differences between them. For one thing, every manager needs to be a leader, but not every leader needs to be a manager.

The leader comes first. Leadership captures concepts, visions, and overall direction. Once those are established, management sees that it is done.

Richard Hutcheson explains leadership as "a function of the *relationship between persons*, those in charge and those who voluntarily follow. Leadership both shapes and is shaped by those who follow. The one thing it *cannot* do is ignore the constituency."[17] Effective church leadership accurately perceives where the people in the congregation are now, and what their potential is for the future. It then takes steps to motivate them to move ahead and become all that God wants them to be. The leader is always out in front, but not too far. The leader sees possibilities that others do not see, and changes the perspective of the church members to fit these possibilities.

Management is different. Ted Engstrom points out that while leadership is based on vision, faith, and concepts, management operates with realistic perspectives, facts, and functions. Leadership cares about effectiveness while management cares about efficiency.[18] Leadership decides where we are going and why. Management figures out how to get there.

I see the difference between leadership and management as relating to a pair of spiritual gifts mentioned in the Bible, namely *leadership* and *administration*. The gift of leadership is mentioned in the list of gifts in Romans 12:8, while administration comes up in another list in 1 Corinthians 12:28. In the original Greek they are two different words.

The word for administration in 1 Corinthians is the Greek word for *helmsman*. In the shipping industry the helmsman is the person who understands the technology of getting the ship from one place to another. The helmsman or manager does some leading in a middle-level sense because the helmsman has to direct the crew and make sure each worker does his or her part in accomplishing the task. But the owner of the ship is the real leader. The owner decides where the ship is to go and what it is going to carry. It is conceivable that the owner of the ship knows very little about navigation or sailing or what to do in a thunderstorm.

I define the two spiritual gifts in question as follows:[19]

Leadership: The gift of leadership is the special ability that God gives to certain members of the Body of Christ to set goals in accordance with God's purpose for the future, and to communicate these goals to others in such a way that they voluntarily and harmoniously work together to accomplish these goals for the glory of God.

Administration: The gift of administration is the special ability that God gives to certain members of the Body of Christ to understand clearly the immediate and long-range goals of a particular unit of the Body of Christ, and to devise and execute effective plans for the accomplishment of those goals.

Few pastors are pure leaders or pure administrators. Most are a mix of the two. But I have observed that pastors who tend toward being leaders, whether or not they also are administrators, will most likely be church growth pastors. Pastors who see themselves to be administrators and use that kind of a management style tend to be maintenance oriented. Making sure that the church as it is functions smoothly and harmoniously is usually where a manager is. A leader, on the other hand, is willing to take risks and upset the status quo in order to move out toward new horizons.

Limitations to Leadership

Let's assume that you have agreed that strong pastoral leadership helps churches grow. Let's assume that you have resolved to ask God to help you become as strong a leader as possible. If so, you will immediately discover that your particular life situation has built-in limitations as to how you will be allowed to lead. There are at least five important sets of factors that in most cases are givens. But within each set of factors you will find strong leaders and weak leaders. I suggest that you try to locate your own life situations in each of the five ranges, and within those limitations attempt to be as strong a leader as possible.

Cultural limitations

Each of us as a human being is a part of a specific culture which predetermines much about our values and behavior patterns and shapes our worldview. There are thousands of major cultures in the world and numerous significant minor variations of them. Part of each cultural context is an intricate system of leadership selection and legitimation. The people who belong to each culture group expect that legitimate leaders will behave in certain manners and that they deserve to be followed to the degree they conform to that kind of behavior. When a church is established within that culture, to a large degree the form which effective church leadership patterns will take is determined by that culture.

As missiologists continually point out, one of the mistakes that missionaries have frequently made in establishing churches in other cultures is to superimpose a system of church government which makes little sense at all to the people. When I was a new missionary in Bolivia I remember well my frustration at what I considered disorganized and inefficient church meetings. So I translated *Robert's Rules of Order* into Spanish thinking it would solve the problem. Just the opposite! Looking back now I can hardly believe my naivete and lack of cultural sensitivity.

Speaking of Latin America, a culturally-relevant leadership pattern which has evolved there is that of the *caudillo*. The *caudillo* is the strong man, the macho, the dictator. Very few Latin American presidents since independence from Spain and Portugal have been voted into office through free elections. They have struggled through the system, been knocked around by competitors, and landed on their feet. Their peers have recognized them as leaders, and they run their government as they see fit.

The fastest growing family of churches in Latin America is the Pentecostals, now numbering over

75 percent of Latin American Protestants. I have spent some time studying the phenomenal growth of these churches, and one of the things I have found is that, in a Christian way, their leadership system follows the pattern of the secular *caudillo*. It is hard for the Latin American leaders themselves to comprehend this when I point it out to them because the *caudillo* is always thought of in the secular world as ruthless, pragmatic, and bloodthirsty. But in the churches the Pentecostals have developed a kind of servant-*caudillo* pattern. Remember the dilemmas? It is possible to be a strong, Christian *caudillo* and be perceived by the people who follow as their servant who truly loves them. The typical Pentecostal pastor of a large growing church in Latin America is exactly that, whether they are conscious of the fact or not.

Now in an African village the *caudillo* is unknown. The culture there has determined that all government will be by consensus. The chief of the village is a very patient man. When an important decision is needed, he will be very sure that there is a full group consensus as to the best way to go before he announces a decision. And it is not surprising that the strong leaders of the growing African churches know how the consensus system operates, and they use it in their churches.

My point is that whether you are working from a *caudillo* model in Latin America or a consensus model in Africa you will find strong leaders and weak leaders, just as you do in America where the democratic, majority rules model is mostly followed.

Missiologist Martin Goldsmith of England suggests that superimposing European and American ideals of democratic leadership style could be a reason for slow growth of churches in Japan. The leader of a European missionary society working in Japan told him that while most churches in Japan were not growing, a few were really growing vigorously, and that typically their lay members were very active for the Lord. But he went on to comment that "the ministers of those churches have become little dictators and we have failed to help them become less autocratic." Goldsmith replied with great wisdom: "Could it be that spiritually minded *autocratic* ministry suits Japan well?" His friend could hardly handle it at first, but he finally admitted that in Japan the political, industrial, and social structures all operate under powerful autocratic leadership styles. Then he became open to seeing that perhaps a democratic leadership, superimposed by missionaries from outside, could be a factor which has *retarded* Japanese church growth through the years.[20]

Socioeconomic limitations

Within many cultures, particularly those in urbanized and industrialized societies, there are several different socioeconomic levels. Leadership patterns can vary significantly from one level to another. In America, for example, trade union members who are high school graduates will generally respond to a leadership style different from that which is relevant to business executives and professionals who hold college degrees. Factory workers respond well to authoritative type leadership, while professionals and middle managers respond better to a participatory style of leadership. These socioeconomic preferences carry over into the churches as well.

For example, my church is Lake Avenue Congregational Church of Pasadena, California. It is a large church with around 3,000 in attendance on a Sunday morning, and it is growing. It happens to be upper middle class socioeconomically. One of the major pieces of equipment is a huge Xerox machine which even collates the printed pages. Because the lay leaders come largely from middle and top management positions, they demand significant study before decisions are made. All options must be thoroughly examined. Detailed reports are needed for major and minor decisions and purchasing paper is a significant church budget item. The pastor, Paul Cedar, is well aware that only a participatory style of leadership will work well in the church. But he is a strong leader who knows where God wants the church to go, who has assumed the responsibility for growth, and who can motivate others to follow him—all within the limitations imposed by his particular congregation.

Much of what our church goes through to make decisions would be considered superfluous in a working class church. "We don't need all that rigamarole!" a deacon might well say. Working class people for the most part do not care to be part of the decision-making process. They feel uncomfortable if they are expected to come up with ideas. They are used to the foreman or the union boss telling them what to do, and they do not resent it in the least. Oh, because they are Americans they like to take a vote on important issues somewhere along the line, but if their pastor is a strong leader who understands the system, there will be little doubt as to how any given congregational vote will come out.

Check out the growing working class churches in your area and you will usually find a pastor who is an autocratic servant-leader. Check out the growing upper-middle to upper class churches and you will usually find a pastor who is a participatory servant-leader. But notice—they are both servants and strong leaders who understand their people and their expectations for leadership.

Denominational limitations

A pastor working within a denominational framework is automatically limited in what can be done by the established polity of the denomination. However, I can think of no denomination which does not include within the boundaries of its polity both strong leaders and weak leaders.

The British, who value the monarchy with all its pomp and circumstance, like bishops and archbishops in church leadership. The Anglican church in England and the Episcopal church in America reflect their culture. Methodists emerged from the Anglican church and retained the bishops. The power is centered in the episcopacy in these churches. It is therefore harder for the pastor of a local parish to be a strong leader than it is in other, more democratic, denominations. Nevertheless, there are very effective Episcopal and Methodist pastors who know how to be strong within the system.

Presbyterians started in Scotland partially as a reaction against the bishops. Consequently, they set up a leadership polity that took power from the bishops and placed it in the hands of the elders of the local congregation. The meeting of the elders is called the session and the pastor, an elder by definition, is the moderator of the session. Here is a denominational government which delivers leadership authority to the pastor on a silver platter, but there are many Presbyterian pastors who despite their polity are weak leaders.

The American democratic ideal is reflected in

the polity of Baptist and Congregational churches. Theoretically the power is in the congregation, and any significant church action can be initiated by any member of the church in a congregational meeting. In large growing Baptist and Congregational churches, however, the center of power has almost invariably been transferred functionally, if not formally, from the congregation to the pastor. When this is done harmoniously, it is a sign that the pastor has been recognized as a servant and that the people trust him or her as their leader. When the congregation refuses to transfer power to the pastor, this decision frequently becomes an obstacle to growth.

Local congregational limitations

Regardless of the denomination it is affiliated with, at least three characteristics of the local congregation in which a pastor is ministering will impose limitations on the type of leadership which will be permitted.

The first is the tradition of the church. If it is a church which places a high value on being run by laypeople, the possibilities of a new pastor changing this are low. One church here in Southern California was founded by a small group of laypeople who became elders for life. The first pastor they called came before traditions were set in concrete and was able to gain a strong leadership position. The church grew remarkably under his ministry with over 2,000 in worship. But since he left a few years ago the church has gone through stormy seas and even a split because it has been impossible for other pastors to come in at this stage and gain permission of the founding elders to lead the church.

The second is related to it. The older a church

the more likely its traditions will not be changed. It is difficult for a pastor to take strong leadership in an old church which has been meeting in the same building for a long time. The exception is a church which for one reason or another is in crisis. For example, Pastor Richard Anderson accepted a call to Sierra Madre Congregational Church in California several years ago. That was an old church with very strong traditions, but it was practically dead. Attendance was down to about twenty-five when they called Anderson. He had permission to go in as a strong leader and has moved the church through a golden age of growth and vitality.

The third characteristic of a local congregation which will limit the role of the pastor is its size. As a rule, the larger the church the more crucial is the role of the senior pastor. The smaller the church the less important is the pastoral leadership. In fact in some small churches important decisions are made and only then the pastor is informed of the decision. And these decisions are typically not made in official board or congregational meetings. They are made on the telephone or in the hay field or over a cup of coffee. Churches which insist on this decision-making process are more than likely to remain small churches. If they are to grow, they need to decide to be led like large churches. There is no question about the pastoral role in large churches. Lyle Schaller calls strong pastoral leadership "the central variable in developing an effective church growth strategy for large congregations." He goes on to say, "The pastor must be willing to accept and fill a strong leadership role and serve as the number-one leader in that congregation."[21]

Personality limitations

The fifth and final limitation on how strong a given pastor's leadership role can be is highly personal. It depends on the temperament of the pastor himself or herself. Some pastors are take-charge people, and some could never bring themselves to take charge. This factor becomes quite important when considering the role of women in the ministry. While some women can take charge, the percentage who can, and who are allowed to by their congregations, is considerably lower than for men.

These personality traits can be changed in some cases, but by and large they are givens which a pastor needs to live with. I myself feel that each of us needs to regard ourselves as a product of God the Creator. He has not created every pastor for pastoring a large, growing church. Some are made to be small-church pastors. In order for us to allow this I mentioned near the beginning of the first chapter that small churches are OK. Not every church can or needs to grow. Churches which, for one reason or another, are going to remain small and not grow need pastors. So if a person's leadership potential is limited by personality traits, he or she might consider this God's leading to vocational fulfillment in a smaller church. Such a decision can certainly glorify God.

Theories of Leadership

The fields of business administration and organizational management have become highly developed in recent years. Textbooks on theories of leadership abound. Before discussing some of them, I would like to state my conclusion. Ted Engstrom, one of America's top leaders in the field, puts it this way: "The appropriate style depends a great deal on the task of the organization, the phase of life of the organization, and the needs of the moment."[22] I think this is extremely important. Flexibility is the word. I have a hard time with a book like *A Theology of Church Leadership* by Lawrence O. Richards and Clyde Hoeldtke (Zondervan Publishing House, 1981) which professes to have located *the* biblically-determined leadership style. My observation is that God blesses many different church leadership styles as long as they are implemented in a Christian way.

The famous German sociologist Max Weber came up with a theory of leadership in the early part of our century which has stood the test of time. It has direct application to church leadership as well as secular. Weber identifies three ways that society legitimizes leadership: legal-rational, traditional, and charismatic. *Legal-rational* leadership is based on what the law dictates and has little to do with the person of the leader who holds the office. The office makes the person and not vice versa. A judge, for example, is not supposed to let his or her personality get in the way of upholding the laws of the land. *Traditional* authority is gained by the leader fitting into the patterns of the system fixed by tradition. A monarchy is set up in this way with the king's son traditionally being the next king. *Charismatic* leadership is gained through the personality of the leader himself or herself. The Latin American *caudillo* whom I recently mentioned is an example of this kind of leadership.

Hardly any leader, secular or in the church, fits entirely into any one of these pure, ideal types. Most are a mixture. But tendencies toward one of the three are usually discernable. You can see how some pastors would fit broadly into one or another of the types. However, leaders of large, growing churches are almost invariably charismatic leaders. They are not strong because of the office they hold or because of the tradition of the church. They are strong because of the power of the Holy Spirit flowing through them. Although Weber doesn't stress this, the word *charisma* is the Greek word for spiritual gift, and as we will see shortly, church growth leadership is strongly gift based.

I find that textbooks on management can become exceedingly complex. Some taxonomies are even three-dimensional, which I personally have a very difficult time relating to. As I have reviewed some of the literature, however, I have identified two continuums that are extremely helpful to keep in mind as you are selecting your style of pastoral leadership. Both pastors and laypeople should be aware of them. Remember that you are also restricted in one way or another by each of the five categories of limitations we looked at earlier.

Authoritative-participatory
Authoritative leadership is also called *directive* and is characterized by low group control. Participatory leadership is nondirective and characterized by high group control. Since it is a continuum, there are numerous points between the two extremes, and few leaders are found at either end. It is helpful to see that either an authoritative or a participatory style can be used for church leadership, depending on the circumstances. Either one can go bad. An authoritative leader can be domineering and manipulative, motivated by a hunger

for power rather than for the good of the people. A participatory leader can be so laissez faire that he or she is no leader at all, and a leaderless organization can wither and die. But they can also be good. The biblical requirements of humility and servanthood can fit well into all points on the continuum.

Task orientation-people orientation

The task-oriented leader places doing ahead of being. The people-oriented leader puts being ahead of doing. In the church neither extreme is helpful, for doing and being are both important. The people must not be treated as simply means toward an end—the end or the goals must be established according to the needs of the people. But on the other side, the people have been brought into the kingdom of God for a purpose, and if this purpose or task is not accomplished, the persons involved are not fulfilled. Generally speaking, however, as I will explain in a later chapter, pastors who lean toward task orientation have a higher potential for leading their church to growth.

Leadership and Growth Potential

As I have frequently said, the main purpose of this book is to relate the various aspects of church leadership to church growth. I think I can best put together the different parts of what has previously been discussed in a diagram (fig. 1).

Notice that the left-hand side of the diagram shows the pastor as the leader of the church. As you move to the right the pastor leads less and less and the congregation leads more and more. I purposely kept the diagonal line from going into the corners because we rarely find the extreme where the pastor does absolutely all of the leading or the

PASTORAL LEADERSHIP ROLES

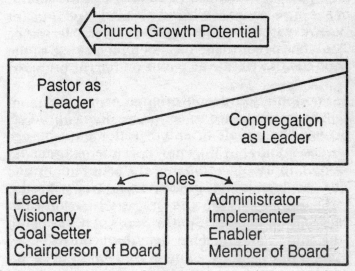

Figure 1

congregation does absolutely all of it. But, as the arrow on the top indicates, the more the tendency goes toward the left with the pastor in strong leadership control, the higher the potential for church growth.

The boxes at the bottom contain descriptions of the leadership roles of the pastor toward one side or the other. Hardly any pastor will check off high on each item on either of the lists—most will find that their profile is complex because of all the limitations—such as cultural, denominational, and personality restrictions.

Nevertheless, the more the pastor can devote time and energy to being a *leader*, rather than an *administrator*, the more growth potential. The leader is not tied down to the nitty-gritty of making the machinery run, but is thinking down the line. The pastor should try to be a *visionary* rather than an *implementer* of someone else's vision. This puts the pastor in the role of a *goal setter* rather than that of an *enabler*. The enabler, as we have previously seen, just sits back and allows the initiative for the future to come from the people in the congregation.

If the particular church or denominational structure allows the pastor to be the *chairperson of the official board*, so much the better. If the pastor is, by church polity, only a *member of the board* (or worse yet, not on the board at all) it is disadvantageous for growth. David Womack says, "I have never yet seen a congregation develop satisfactorily for long if its pastor was not the leader of the church and the chairman of the board .... I would not pastor a church if I could not be its leader, and I would not advise any pastor to accept such a position of nonbiblical organization."[23] He goes on to point out that in New Testament times the deacons were not chosen to be a board of directors over the ministers.

The model I have presented is a very strong model, and it can easily be misunderstood at this point. The next chapter will help balance it. It is not my intention to leave the people of the congregation out of the picture. When Ralph H. Elliott, one of the sharpest critics of the Church Growth Movement, came to this part of the church growth theory, he understood me to say that rather than sharing pastoral duties with church members, "the pastor as administrative leader is encouraged to abdicate all such responsiblities."[24] What I really intended to promote is maximizing the role of the laypeople of the church in ministry, but at the same time maximizing the role of the pastor in leadership. Up to this point we have dealt mainly with the leadership; the ministry will come later.

Where Does This Leadership Come From?

If strong pastoral leadership is as important for church growth as it seems, then many by now are asking, how can I become a strong leader? There are three major sources of leadership. I like to say it is earned, it is discerned, and it is learned.

Leadership is earned

The final test of leadership, as I have said before, is that there be followers. Since charismatic leadership is so important in the church, it follows that it is not automatic that people will follow a pastor just because he or she has the title. When you accept a call to an existing church you are on probation usually for three to six years. During that period of time, the people in the church are in the process of deciding one thing above all—whether or not you are their servant. This is what is behind Lyle Schaller's observation that the productive years of a given pastorate *begin* around years four, five, or six. It takes that long to earn your right to lead by proving that you are a servant.

Once the people believe that you are their servant, you will gain their full love and trust. Then the sky's the limit as far as your leadership possibilities are concerned. Paul Yonggi Cho, pastor of the world's largest church, says, "The members of Full Gospel Central Church obey me because they know I genuinely love them." He goes on to say that Christians who do not respect their pastor are wrong because "the pastor has been anointed by God to lead the sheep." However, it is not automatic because the pastor "has to show real Christlike love to the sheep before they will follow him unreservedly."[25] This is Cho's way of saying that leadership must be earned.

Leadership is discerned

As I have studied large growing churches I have discovered that their pastors all seem to have two of the spiritual gifts: faith and leadership. They are very closely related. I defined leadership a few pages back as setting goals in accordance with God's purpose for the future of the church and motivating others to contribute toward the accomplishment of the goals. But how does a pastor know for sure what is God's purpose for the church? Through the gift of faith. The gift of faith is the special ability that God gives to certain members of the Body of Christ to discern with extraordinary confidence the will and purposes of God for the future of His work.

Spiritual gifts, in my view, are not ordered up or achieved by good works. They are received through the grace of God, and our responsibility is to discern which gift or gifts God has given us. Then we are to develop them and use them for His glory. God chooses some of His servants to receive the gifts of faith and leadership. I will elaborate on how they work together for effective goal setting in a later chapter, but here we need to recognize that they do exist. The gift of leadership is mentioned in Romans 12:8 and faith is in 1 Corinthians 12:9.

Leadership is learned

No matter where you are as a leader today, you can be a stronger leader by taking appropriate training. If you have the gift of leadership, you need to develop that gift to your greatest potential. And if you don't have the gift, you can still be a reasonably competent leader, although it will not be as easy. Your personality has placed certain limitations on your leadership ability, but even your personality can be changed to a certain degree through training and therapy.

Learning more about the dynamics of church growth will also help you be a better growth leader. Expertise in a field carries built-in authority. If your people see that you have the knowledge skills to lead their church to growth, they follow. And this knowledge is available through books, tapes, seminars, and academic courses. In fact if you do not become a better leader just through reading this book, I will be disappointed.

Notes

1. Richard G. Hutcheson, Jr., *The Wheel Within the Wheel: Confronting the Management Crisis of the Pluralistic Church* (Atlanta: John Knox Press, 1979), p. 54.

2. Lyle E. Schaller, *Effective Church Planting* (Nashville: Abingdon Press, 1979), p. 162.

3. Hutcheson, *Wheel Within the Wheel*, p. 53.

4. Schaller, *Effective Church Planning*, pp. 162-163.

5. Hutcheson, *Wheel Within the Wheel*, p. 57.

6. *Ibid.*

7. Schaller, *Effective Church Planning*, p. 163.

8. Robert C. Girard, *Brethren, Hang Loose* (Grand Rapids: Zondervan Publishing House, 1972), pp. 209-210.

9. David Mains, "My Greatest Ministry Mistakes," *Leadership*, Spring, 1980, p. 20.

10. Jackson W. Carroll and Robert L. Wilson, *Too Many Pastors? The Clergy Job Market* (New York: Pilgrim Press, 1980), p. 118.

11. D. Dewayne Davenport, *The Bible Says Grow: Church Growth Guidelines for Church of Christ* (Williamstown, WV: Church Growth/Evangelism Seminar, 1978), p. 35.

12. Jack Hayford, "Servant Leadership," *The Pentecostal Minister*, Spring, 1983, p. 12.

13. *Ibid.*, p. 13.

14. Jack W. Hayford, *The Church on the Way* (Lincoln, VA: Chosen Books, 1982), p. 22.

15. Gordon MacDonald, "Ten Conditions for Church Growth," *Leadership*, Winter, 1983, pp. 44-48.

16. Lawrence O. Richards, *Three Churches in Renewal* (Grand Rapids: Zondervan Publishing House, 1975), p. 44.

17. Hutcheson, *Mainline Churches*, p. 158.

18. Ted W. Engstrom, *The Making of a Christian Leader* (Grand Rapids: Zondervan Publishing House, 1976), p. 23.

19. For definitions of the twenty-seven spiritual gifts see my book *Your Spiritual Gifts Can Help Your Church Grow* (Bromley: MARC Europe, 1985), pp. 259-263.

20. Martin Goldsmith, *Can My Church Grow?* (London: Hodder & Stoughton, 1980), pp. 55-56.

21. Lyle E. Schaller, *Growing Plans* (Nashville: Abingdon Press, 1983), p. 85.

22. Engstrom, *The Making of a Christian Leader*, p. 78.

23. David A. Womack, *The Pyramid Principle of Church Growth* (Minneapolis: Bethany Fellowship, 1977), p. 90.

24. Ralph H. Elliott, *Church Growth That Counts* (Valley Forge: Judson Press, 1982), p. 82.

25. Paul Yonggi Cho, *Successful Home Cell Groups* (Plainfield, NJ: Logos International, 1981), pp. 94-95.

4

The Fine Art of Lay Followership

It seems rather strange that very few books on leadership have chapters on followership. As a matter of fact, *followership* is not even in the unabridged dictionary. There seems to be a curious assumption that while leaders need special instruction for exercising their role, followers need no such instruction.

The more I study church leadership, the more I disagree with the assumption. Many pastors who would like to, cannot lead their congregation because of a basic lack of sensitivity on the part of the people as to their role as followers. A good starting point for looking into the followership role of the people of God is the Bible. What does it have to say?

Leadership and Followership in Scripture
When the Bible touches on the matter of Christian leadership it supports a strong leadership role for the pastor. One of the first things you discover in making a study of leadership in the Bible is that you are not forced into any one rigid pattern of

leadership that is to be applied to all churches everywhere. In fact, many scholars have traced the variations in leadership patterns that we see in the Jewish churches in Jerusalem, then how they changed in earlier Gentile churches, then how they continued to change in the later Gentile churches. All of them had "New Testament leadership," but they were different.

The two words in Greek most used to describe leaders are the word for elder, *presbuteros*, from which the Presbyterian church derives its name, and the word for overseer or bishop, *episkopos*, from which the Episcopal church gets its name. The elder is literally an older person, respected by the public for maturity and wisdom. The bishop is one who takes oversight of a church and serves as its chief executive officer. The word for pastor or shepherd, *poimen*, is also used in the New Testament to signify the responsibility that a church leader has for the spiritual well-being of a determined group of God's people. Other terms are used such as *leader* (Rom. 12:8), *administrator* (1 Cor. 12:28), "those . . . over you in the Lord" (1 Thess. 5:12), "those who have rule over you" (Heb. 13:7), and "leading men" (Acts 15:22). None of these terms is used in a technical sense. They seem to be interchangeable. In 1 Peter 5:1-2, for example, the concepts of elder, pastor, and bishop all refer to the same leaders of the church.

I agree with Michael Griffiths who says of the biblical teaching on leadership, "The only general conclusion is that, while there is always officially recognized authority and leadership which is to be respected and obeyed, the actual titles used and the mode of organization are quite different."[1] Denominational leaders will often defend their own governmental system as being more biblical than others, but the arguments are frequently academic. Most of the structures that I am aware of are equally biblical because the Bible is broad enough to include them all. The only position I would disagree with is the one which says that a particular church government is the *only* biblical one and all others are either nonbiblical or sub-biblical.

Notice that Michael Griffiths mentioned that biblical leadership is intended "to be respected and obeyed." This is what I am calling *follower-ship.* When we look a little more closely at the key biblical passages on leadership we can immediately see that both strong leadership and obedient followership are consistently taught.

In order to do this, I want to identify the role verbs in four key leadership passages. Then I will list the verbs which apply to the pastor or church leader in one column and those which apply to the people of the congregation in another. The first step is to look at the passages with the role verbs emphasized by capital letters.

John 10:2-4: "He who ENTERS BY THE DOOR is the shepherd of the sheep. To him the door-keeper opens, and the sheep HEAR HIS VOICE; and he CALLS HIS OWN SHEEP BY NAME and LEADS THEM OUT. And when he brings out his own sheep, he GOES BEFORE THEM; and the sheep FOLLOW HIM, for they KNOW HIS VOICE."

1 Thessalonians 5:12-13: "And we urge you, brethren, to RECOGNIZE those who LABOR among you, and ARE OVER YOU in the Lord and ADMONISH YOU, and to ESTEEM THEM very highly IN LOVE for their work's sake. BE AT PEACE among yourselves."

Hebrews 13:17: "OBEY those who RULE over you, and be SUBMISSIVE, for they WATCH OUT

FOR YOUR SOULS, as those who must GIVE ACCOUNT. LET THEM DO SO WITH JOY and not with grief, for that would be unprofitable for you."

1 Peter 5:2-3: "SHEPHERD the flock of God which is among you, SERVING AS OVERSEERS, not by constraint but willingly, not for dishonest gain but eagerly; NOR AS BEING LORDS over those ENTRUSTED TO YOU, but BEING EXAMPLES to the flock."

Role verbs for the pastor	Role verbs for the people
the shepherd:	the sheep:
enters by the door	hear his voice
calls his sheep by name	follow him
leads them out	know his voice
goes before them	
those who labor among you:	brethren:
labor	recognize them
are over you	esteem them
admonish you	love them
	be at peace
those who have rule:	Hebrew believers:
have rule	obey
watch out for souls	submit
give account	let them do it with joy
the elders among you:	the flock:
shepherd	entrusted to the pastor
serve as overseers	
not being lords	
being examples	

It takes less than thirty seconds to look up and down those two columns and to be deeply impressed with the seriousness of biblical leadership and followership. It is the followership teaching which has most been neglected in our churches and which I am stressing in this chapter. One of the reasons I think it has been neglected is that most pastors have an extremely difficult time teaching this explicitly. I can say many things in a book like this that would be inappropriate for a pastor to say to a congregation unless there were a substantial background of deep mutual understanding. If a pastor ever has to cajole or beg or threaten a congregation in order to gain leadership, it is a sure indication that he or she does not have it and will probably never get it. As John Bisagno says, "You do not have to ask for leadership . . . . When you have to start reminding them that you are the pastor, you no longer are!"[2]

But this did not keep the apostles who wrote the New Testament from instructing Christians how to be good followers. Church members are "entrusted" by God to their pastor just as sheep on the farm are. The sheep do not tell the pastor where to go; they trust the pastor to lead them into green pastures. Phillip Keller, a sheep farmer himself and author of the best-selling book *A Shepherd Looks at Psalm 23,* points out that sheep do not "just take care of themselves." He says, "They require, more than any other class of livestock, endless attention and meticulous care."[3] The welfare of sheep is uniquely dependent on the shepherd. "Under one man," says Keller, "sheep would struggle, starve and suffer endless hardship. In another's care they would flourish and thrive contentedly."[4]

This can also be applied to your church, which is called a "flock" by the Bible. God is the one who sets a pastor over a local church. This is why a pastor usually refers to "my call to the church." The call came through the appointed representatives of the congregation or through the bishop as the case may be, but in either case the invitation to serve the church is based on an indispensable assumption: that the originator of the "call" was God. It is presumed that God led both the pastor and the human agent through which the particular call came. That is why Peter says that the flock is "entrusted" to the pastor who should serve as "overseer." It is God's own plan for the church.

Church members are told to "recognize" their pastors. Pastors should not only be invited to serve a congregation, but they should be given the responsibility to lead and the authority to commensurate with the responsibility. They should be given the title they deserve. A close pastor friend of mine had served a prominent church for over a year with a considerable amount of frustration. I recall the day he said to me with an exasperated grin on his face, "Someone finally referred to me as the senior pastor the other day." Needless to say, he soon resigned. The people of the church, particularly the elders, were not ready to recognize their pastor as leader.

Lyle Schaller sees this as a modern trend. He says, "We've been dealing for twenty-five years with the devaluation of pastors."[5] One of the symptoms is the tendency to ignore pastors' anniversaries. Many more churches used to celebrate the anniversary of the pastor's call. Black churches still do, but white churches do not so much. Schaller feels that this has had a psychological impact on pastors, making pastors feel their role is less important. I think this is true, and if it is, it undoubtedly is a cause of slow growth in many churches and even denominations. Furthermore, it is not biblical because congregations are told to "recognize" their pastors.

They are also told to "esteem" their pastors. Few people recognize how strong this biblical term is: "esteem them very highly" (1 Thess. 5:13). Leon Morris's commentary says, "[Paul's] adverb 'exceedingly highly' is a very expressive and emphatic compound, found in this precise form here only in the New Testament."[6] The corollaries of this are to "obey" and "submit," very strong verbs in our day of anti-authoritarianism and in our democratic culture. All this is to be done, not grudgingly but "in love." Do you and your fellow church members love your pastor? If not there is something wrong. True, there may be something wrong with the pastor, but there's an equal possibility that there may be something wrong with you. When love is prominent, the rest will follow: you will be "at peace among yourselves" and your pastor will be leading "with joy." According to Hebrews 13:17, a layperson who is causing his or her pastor grief is out of the will of God.

Why should the Scriptures go to such a length to describe Christian followership? In the plan of God the flock is to be "entrusted" to the pastor and the pastor is to "give account." If Jesus, the "Chief Shepherd" (1 Pet. 5:4) returns today, the first person He will call to give an account of your church will be the pastor. True, every single member will also be asked to report their church activities, but no one—elders, deacons, trustees or Sunday School teachers—will be called before the pastor. Laypeople who take this seriously tend to develop appropriate followership skills.

Leadership, Not Lordship

In this series of biblical passages, one sharp warning is sounded for pastors. A great deal of leadership authority is handed to them, but because they are human beings this can be, and all too often is, abused. Peter says that pastors should not lead by "constraint," they should not lead for "dishonest gain," and they should not be "lords" (1 Pet. 5:2-3). The dishonest gain I will discuss later. Right here I want to deal with the possibility that a given pastor will rule with constraint and become a lord rather than a leader.

This takes us back to an item from the last chapter. Jesus was explaining to His disciples the dilemma between leadership and servanthood sparked by an illegitimate request from James and John. When Jesus got to glory, one of them wanted to be seated on His right hand and one on His left. Jesus compared this request to the way the rulers of the Gentiles "lord it over them" and "exercise authority over them" (Mark 10:42). In the terminology of Max Weber, they wanted to be awarded legal-rational leadership. Jesus refused it and told them in effect that Christian leadership needed to be charismatic leadership, and that they could only gain this recognition through servanthood.

In the secular world, referred to as the "Gentiles," authority is exercised through a coercive use of power. Those who hold certain positions can force others to do what they want them to do. They can threaten to fire them or to demote them or to give them unpleasant work or to refuse them a raise. Leaders in the secular world find ways and means of manipulating people for their own ends. They are tyrants. This is lordship, not leadership, and Jesus says, "It shall not be so among you" (Mark 10:43).

Sociologically, churches are voluntary associations. Spiritually, churches are the family of God. Neither allows for a coercive type of leadership authority. Pastors who do not understand this find themselves in trouble. They need to remember that they are servants, and what they do has to be with the consent of the followers and for their good. A happy relationship between the pastor and the people is essential in the church. The people will know intuitively whether or not the pastor loves them. It is a feeling produced by the Holy Spirit Himself within the church. The secular world knows nothing about this, but the church can't get along without it. Pastor Paul Yonggi Cho, one of the strongest Christian leaders I know, says, "In our church we have 'authority with love.' If a pastor really loves the people in his congregation, they will respond to his authority and obey his teaching." That is Cho's description of Christian leadership. Then he goes on to describe lordship: "But if the pastor tries to exert his authority merely on the strength of his position or on human maneuvering, the people will rebel and he will be in trouble."[7]

The thing that a church desiring to grow needs to pray for is a pastor who is both a charismatic leader and a servant. There is no reason to hide the fact that many charismatic leaders do not fulfill the servanthood requirement and fall into the temptation to become lords over the congregation. Natural born enabler types are not usually tempted along those lines. After studying ten of America's fastest growing churches, Elmer Towns found that they were characterized by charismatic pastoral leadership, but that the very nature of that leadership style runs the danger of having it degenerate into authoritarianism. Towns feels that a leader should be *authoritative* without being *authoritarian*. The difference often depends on the locus of power. "When the pastor realizes he is an undershepherd, receiving his authority from the Word of God, he gives an *authoritative* leadership to his church. When the pastor localizes power in his personality, he gives *authoritarian* leadership to the church."[8] Towns distinguishes very well between lordship and leadership.

Defending Against Lordship

The dangers of lordship, rather than Christian leadership, are clear. I have heard numerous stories of bad experiences with tyrant-pastors from lay leaders in almost every denomination. Some congregations have been so badly burned by unloving and manipulative pastors that they have built rather elaborate defense mechanisms to prevent it from happening again in the future. This would be all right, but unfortunately the steps they have taken have often created another problem—they have erected a barrier to church growth. In most cases the people have never even imagined that there would be a negative outcome of their actions, because they are concentrating so intensely on solving the immediate problem of pastor-people relationships.

At least three common situations arise from people defending themselves against pastors who exercise lordship rather than leadership. They take it out on the next pastor, they shift the power to the elders, or they shift the power to the congregation. Let's look at them one at a time.

Taking it out on the next pastor

I feel sorry for church growth pastors who accept a call to a church which has just been burned by a careless and insensitive tyrant-pastor. The risk in a church like that is high, especially if the new pastor is ignorant of the feelings of the people. As Elmer Towns observes, "Because some pastors swing to one extreme, the lay leaders strip the next pastor of the ability to lead . . . . Many churches handcuff the gifted pastor and do not give him the freedom to lead the flock."[9]

There is no question that at times a church needs a period of healing, and during that time not much growth can be expected. An interim pastor is often very helpful to a church which has been hurt. But we must be reminded that this is a book focusing on church growth. The tendency for a church going through a healing process is to focus on congregational peace and harmony and lose the vision for growth. "We need to get better before we get bigger" is the common phrase heard in board meetings. But the process of getting better never ends, and growth is often forgotten. Churches that feel hurt because of the wrong kind of strong leadership should look for the right kind of strong leadership if they are to grow. As Elmer Towns says, "The Bible recognizes the gifted man and teaches that the greater the man, the greater the results."[10] I recall hearing G. L. Johnson, pastor of People's Church in Fresno, California, say, "If the pastor's a winner the church will be a winner; if the pastor's a loser the church will be a loser." This is true, and is one reason that congregations which have gone through an unfortunate situation with a pastor need to rise above it and trust God for a sensitive servant-leader who also has a vision for growth and knows how to take the kind of authority that will accomplish it.

Shifting the power to the elders

The succession of leadership from one pastor to the next is usually an immediate set of circumstances which can be corrected and resolved fairly easily. No one has claimed that "the Bible says we must take it out on the next pastor." Shifting the power from the pastor to the elders, however, is another story. In some cases it has been the result of a long process of church history and has been encased in denominational tradition. Also, some nondenominational churches, founded by elders who did not appreciate strong pastoral leadership, have written it into their constitution and bylaws. In order to justify this, it has often been strongly theologized and once that happens it is difficult to change.

The basic motivations for establishing a plurality of elders as the ideal form of church leadership are good. For one thing it creates checks and balances so that no one person could ever be a tyrant even if he or she wanted to be one. Secondly, it avoids clericalism in which all the ministry of the church is seen to be concentrated in the person of the pastor. The third is the flip side of the second, namely a desire to free the laypeople of the church for their own areas of ministry. I could not agree more with those motivations.

There is a danger, however. If all the elders are leaders, no one is a leader. In theory, each elder has equal authority and makes his or her contribution according to the spiritual gifts that God has given to each. Some will teach, some will preach, some will administer, some will counsel, some will visit the hospital. In many plurality-of-elder churches one of them is designated as "pastor/teacher." This is usually the person who would ordinarily be regarded as the senior pastor in more traditional churches, but the title is never awarded. Such a person will almost invariably make the public statement, "Oh, I don't lead the church. The elders do." That sounds like a thoroughly biblical statement to those who have bought into the system.

There are several comments I want to make about shifting the power in the church from the pastor to the elders. First, the idea of freeing all the people in the church to do the work of the ministry is crucial for church growth. But this need not be seen as something incompatible with strong pastoral leadership. Precisely at the point of confusing ministry with leadership is where many have gone astray. One of the major theses of this book is that the two go together and they are both positive church growth factors.

Second, the plurality-of-elders structure is good for small churches and nongrowing churches. But as a church gains growth momentum and becomes larger, the system becomes more dysfunctional. Gene Getz of Fellowship Bible Church in Dallas, Texas, found this out. They started with a group of eight elders who met regularly and ran the church by consensus. However the church grew tremendously and soon there were forty elders. Consensus was no longer possible and Getz sees that in reality it had become a "sloppy voting system." They were actually asking only for negative rather than positive votes and they "had no way to make decisions and move ahead." They finally decided to take votes and allow the freedom to agree to disagree. "As the church grows," Getz says, "it has to take on elements of centralization (as much as I hate the word)."[11] As I have previously mentioned, the larger the church the more crucial is the role of the senior pastor.

Third, I have observed that in almost all of the plurality-of-elders churches which are growing, a top leader has emerged even though one was not supposed to. Some of the strongest leaders I know say "I don't lead" and go ahead and do it. There is a gap between the formal and the functional, between the theory and the practice. This should actually fit the theory of advocates of plural leadership because one of the spiritual gifts presumably given to some elders is that of "leader" (Rom. 12:8). The Greek word used there is *proistemi* which means "to go before." There are other Greek words meaning to go alongside of, but they are not this word. An elder with the leadership gift should be freed to lead. Michael Harper, who agrees that the elders should rule the church, nevertheless sees that "if every society needs leadership and leadership needs to be in the hands of a team, then every team requires a captain." He does not feel that this violates the plurality of eldership principle, "for such a leader is always *primus inter pares.*"[12] Gene Getz reinforces this when he says, "What upsets many people is the claim by some that certain successful churches don't have such a leader. I maintain they all do. He may be 'laid back' in style, but he still leads."[13]

The Churches of Christ and other branches of the Restoration Movement are some of the staunchest advocates of the plurality of elders. That is why I was surprised when I read what one of their leaders, D. Dewayne Davenport, has to say about leadership in a book of his called *The Bible Says Grow: Church Growth Guidelines for Church of Christ.* Davenport admits that what he says "may seem controversial to many readers," but he observes that there is a consensus among Churches of Christ researchers that a major factor of nongrowth is the leadership. Yet "we have some of the greatest men on earth as elders, deacons and preachers in the Churches of Christ." He suggests that the problem may not be so much in the persons themselves as in the organizational structure.

So his conclusion is that in modern days the structural guidelines set up by the founders of the Restoration Movement have not been followed and that many of today's churches are off track. "The main place we jumped the track," asserts Davenport, "is in the role of the preacher and his relationship to the elders. The Bible teaches that the preacher/minister is to take the lead in the local congregation."[14] Davenport's "preacher/minister" of course is the person who in more traditional churches carries the title of senior pastor, but that title is not acceptable in his denomination. Whether they have the title or not the growing churches have the leader. Davenport says, "Just look around and see which churches are growing, then take a look at the leadership of the preacher. In a growing congregation, you will find godly elders who are willing to let the preacher become the leader God intended him to be."[15]

The plurality-of-elders system will work for a large growing church as long as one of them leads. Presbyterians believe in a plurality of elders, but one of them is a teaching elder called the pastor who is designated moderator of the session. Those Presbyterian ministers who are also strong leaders know how to use this position to the benefit of the church. Notice that the elders are also leaders in a middle-management sense of the word. The pastor delegates important leadership responsibilities to the elders. But there is only one top leader in the organization. As Davenport says, "Does this mean the elders are inferior to the preacher? Not at all! They simply let him take the leadership." He then shows how the Madison Church of Christ in Madison, Tennessee, has become the largest church in their brotherhood because, for one thing, "The Madison elders don't think of themselves as 'over' or superior to their preacher. To them God's work is a partnership. They know that God has given Ira North the gift of leadership and they permit him to use it."[16]

Shifting the power to the congregation

Another historical way of avoiding the possibility that the senior pastor will be a tyrant and exercise lordship rather than leadership is to shift the power from the pastor to the congregation. The idea of the congregation leading the church made good headway in America with its democratic ideals. Many denominations, such as Congregationalists and Baptists, follow the principle that the final decision-making entity is the congregation. The pastor serves at the request of the congregation, and in some cases is reminded of this by an annual vote to see if his or her call will be renewed for another year.

I myself am a Congregationalist and have been able to observe the system at fairly close range. I find that the congregational movement is fine for small, uncomplicated churches. It provides built-in checks and balances so that power cannot be abused. But as the church grows it gets more and more unwieldy. As many Congregational churches grow they tend to multiply boards and committees *ad infinitum*. If not held in check, each board or committee can gain policy-making authority for the whole church, much of this in overlapping areas of church life. Leaderlessness drags down the church. The congregational meeting in large Congregational churches is often the most boring meeting in the program because policies have already been made at the various other power centers and the congregation is just a formal rubber stamp for them. In some it is practically impossible even to get a quorum for the business meeting.

Leadership power has long since been drained from the congregation in large Congregational churches. Where is it located? In most of the churches which are no longer growing it is in one or more of the boards or committees. Sometimes it is in the nominating committee. Sometimes it is in the trustees. Sometimes it is in an informal leadership network that channels through certain personalities. On the other hand, in Congregational churches *which are growing*, the power is usually in the pastor. The pastor has long since discovered how to maintain the integrity of the formal congregational government while functioning as a strong leader.

In any church government structure the congregation needs substantial input. This can come through annual meetings, quarterly meetings, or elected representation. In my opinion the ideal structure for large, growing churches is a one-board government; with the pastor serving as chairperson of the board. If the board is representative of the congregation as a whole, the pastor can keep in touch with the feelings of the people through the board. Because of long traditions to the contrary, this structure is not always possible in certain denominations, even though it is ideal. Lyle E. Schaller suggests that in large churches the governing body contain not more than two dozen members, and if it does have more, a strong executive committee should be formed to facilitate the decision-making process.[17]

While the power in the hands of the pastor can

be abused, so can the power in the hands of the congregation. Several illustrations of this are given when the people of Israel rebelled against their leader, Moses. In one of the incidents, Korah's rebellion, an official delegation representing the congregation came to Moses and Aaron. Here is their logic: "You have gone too far! The whole community is holy, every one of them, and the Lord is with them. Why then do you set yourselves above the Lord's assembly?" (Num. 16:3, *NIV*). The obvious answer to the rhetorical question was that Moses did not set himself up, but God did. This is the same with legitimate local church leadership. "He Himself gave some to be ... pastors ... for the equipping of the saints for the work of ministry" (Eph. 4:11-12). Pastors are pastors because God made them to be pastors. Congregations, even those which have a congregational government, need to recognize this biblical truth.

Getting Rid of a Pastor

I have mentioned checks and balances several times. While I believe in strong pastoral leadership I do not believe in autocratic leadership. The pastor must be accountable to the congregation directly or indirectly because he or she is the servant of the congregation. Pastors will frequently refer to "the church that I *serve*." Effective leadership can only be sustained if there is a clear mutual understanding that the pastor knows, understands, and acts in accordance with the needs and desires of the congregation.

Sometimes the pastor goes bad. Unethical conduct and immorality can come into the picture. Power-grabbing and disregard for the feelings of the congregation can cause irreconcilable differences between the pastor and the people. At this point the shepherd analogy breaks down. If somehow literal sheep come under the care of an irresponsible shepherd, they can get sick and die or be devoured by wild beasts. This need not happen to God's people. They are human beings, they are intelligent, and they are made in the image of God. They have the ability to recognize a leader whom, for one reason or another, they cannot follow. If the church is to grow, that leader needs to be changed. In some denominations, the authorities of the judicatory or the denomination can help fire the pastor. In other churches, the responsibility is squarely on the members of the congregation. Unpleasant as the task might be, it has to be done and the quicker the better.

Is Strong Leadership the American Way?

Whenever church growth studies are made questions of cultural bias must be raised. To this point the contents of this book have been directed toward an American audience with mostly American illustrations and applications. However my field is that of international church growth, and over the years I have been interested in testing leadership hypotheses in other cultures as well. For one thing, it seems that if strong pastoral leadership is as biblical as I have been contending, it should be a transcultural principle. I suppose there are exceptions as there are to any other church growth principle, but on the whole the evidence from other parts of the world is that strong leadership also helps churches grow there.

As I discuss church growth I find myself using more and more illustrations from Korea. Korea is one of the flash point regions of worldwide church growth these days. The largest Methodist, Presbyterian, and Assemblies of God churches in the world are already in Korea, and I would expect churches of some other denominations to follow suit. The Full Gospel Central Church, pastored by Paul Yonggi Cho and now running over 300,000 members is the world's largest. Cho appears regularly on American television and some of his books are available in English. If he is representative of Korean pastors, the indication comes loud and clear that Koreans respond well to strong pastoral leadership.

I have already referred to Martin Goldsmith's observation that in Japanese political, industrial and social units a pyramid-type structure with powerful leadership at the top is considered proper. And he suggests that strong, even autocratic, leadership might be good for Japanese church growth.[18] This is reinforced in a Ph.D. dissertation by John Merwin on the holiness church in Japan. Merwin says, "As with all growing churches in Japan, capable pastors are a key factor."[19] And Lavern Snider, after thoroughly studying eight growing churches in Japan, says, "In each of the churches the pastor plays a prominent role, that of spiritual and administrative leader. A congregation's progress or lack of it usually reflects the kind of leadership given by the pastor."[20]

Other illustrations can be brief. Allen Swanson says that in Taiwan, "When God wants to build His church, He always begins with a man—a man with a vision and a burden, a man with a deep desire to honor the Lord, a passion to lead others to Him and to follow the principles of church growth found in the New Testament."[21] Clarence Lim in a study of church growth in Singapore says, "The important factor that determines church growth or decline is its leadership."[22] From Guatemala, Mardoqueo Munoz says, "The role of the pastor is exceedingly crucial in the life of the church."[23] Gordon Moyes, pastor of Australia's largest church, Wesley Central Mission in Sydney, affirms that "the minister is the key person in a growing church . . . All growing churches have a strong ministry."[24]

But back to the U.S.A. With the large and growing number of ethnic groups in America, one needs to ask whether strong pastoral leadership is typical only of our white Anglo-American churches or if it makes sense to other groups. It seems that strong pastoral leadership has never been in question in American black churches. Joseph H. Jackson who was president of the nation's largest black denomination for almost thirty years, said that one reason for his longevity was his respect for pastors. "Every pastor's a king," Jackson said, "and you don't mess with his crown." In an excellent book on black church administration, Massey and McKinney say, "The pastor is commander-in-chief by virtue of his call by God and the people, and often by virtue of his training. For the pastor not to assert himself is a sign of weakness. The 'humble' pastor in past years often found the reins of leadership removed from him."[25] Similar reports, although perhaps not quite as strongly worded, are coming in from other American ethnic groups.

A growing body of evidence seems to confirm the notion that because strong pastoral leadership and committed lay followership are biblical teachings, they play key roles in church growth the world around.

Getting the Congregation Ready for Growth

If the pastor is ready to lead and the congregation is ready to follow, the church has high growth potential. However growth usually doesn't happen by itself, and one of the first steps to make it happen is to get the congregation in the mood for growth.

The first thing to do is to take stock of how ready the congregation is for growth. Lyle Schaller has given us some helpful suggestions for measuring tools. Here are four you can use fairly easily:

Measure the median tenure for members. How long, on the average, have the people belonged to the church? If it is under seven years, you are in good shape for growth. If it is over twelve years, growth will not be easy.

Measure the median tenure for the laypeople who have emerged as the policymakers or legitimizers of policy. If they have longer tenure in the church than the average for members, it is a signal that new people are not now being absorbed into the church as well as they could. More work will be needed for growth.

Measure attendance trends at the worship service. If trends are on the increase, growth will be easier.

Measure the age of the institution. The older the church, the more effort will be required to move into a growth program.[26]

The results of these measurements will simply give you some indication as to what lies ahead. They are not to be used to predict growth or non-growth, but to get a scope of the task. Even if the answers show negative tendencies toward growth, the situation can be changed. I have three suggestions for action toward preparing the congregation for growth:

Make sure the people know their purpose

Unselfishness is right at the essence of the Christian life. Christian people need to be reminded that if they enjoy their relationship to Christ and to each other, they should be reaching out and sharing that blessing with others. In the first chapter I argued strongly for a biblical and theological rationale why churches should grow. Communicate this to the people through sermons and through teaching in Sunday School and in other groups. Show your congregation some of the many excellent church growth films over a period of time.[27] Spend some time one-on-one with key opinion makers of the church, talking about the long-range plans for the church.

It is all too easy for a congregation to become overly comfortable with themselves and the status quo. One of the responsibilities of the pastor is to persuade such a complacent congregation that God desires much more for them.

Make sure they are in touch with God

Church growth does not happen merely as the result of human efforts. Jesus said, "I will build my church." He is the one who is doing it, using humans as His instruments. It is therefore necessary that the people of the church be in close touch with God, and it is the pastor's responsibility to see that this happens.

In some churches there will be a significant number of church members who are not committed to Christ. They are part of the church life, but they have never been born again. They may know about God but they do not really know Him. They are not in personal touch with the power of the Holy Spirit. Leading such persons to a full commitment to Jesus Christ needs to be a high priority item when it is a problem.

Assuming that the people in the church do relate to Jesus Christ as their personal Saviour and Lord, cultivate a prayer life for the unchurched. I will say more about spiritual formation in a later chapter, but I'll mention now that there seems to be an encouraging trend in the United States toward a more active and meaningful life of prayer among Christian people. While more research needs to be done to determine the relationship of prayer to church growth, most church growth leaders have strong intuitive feelings that there is more cause-and-effect relationship than we think.

Make sure their morale is high

Pastor Charles Mylander of Rose Drive Friends Church in Yorba Linda, California, says that "high morale is essential for a growing church." My observations confirm this. There is an electricity in a growing church that simply is not present in plateaued or nongrowing churches. Mylander also points out that the effect is cyclical: "High morale is conducive to church growth, which results in higher morale, which encourages greater growth, and so on."[28] His three principles of morale building are worth keeping in mind. First, morale builds through a contagious sense of expectancy. A relationship of love, respect, and enthusiasm between pastor and people is at the heart of this. Second, morale builds through a series of good experiences. Unselfishness of the people as reflected in giving is a key part. And finally, morale builds through God-given achievement. Setting goals and reaching them produce a highly contagious attitude toward growth.[29]

Lay Ministry and Growth Potential

The stage, presumably, is set. The pastor is a strong leader who wants the church to grow and is willing to pay the price. The people of the congregation are aware of their biblical role of followership and are willing to allow their pastor to lead. The congregation as a whole is motivated for growth. Now comes the hard work.

The chief contribution of laypeople to the growth of the church can be summed up in one word: ministry. This is taught clearly in the Bible. Pastors, along with other leaders such as apostles, prophets, evangelists and teachers, were given by God to the church for the specific function of: "equipping of the saints for the work of the ministry" (Eph. 4:12). The saints, of course, are the people of God, the members of the church. Every church member is supposed to be an active minister. That is why I prefer the word *pastor* for the person who leads the church rather than *minister,* although I would not want to quarrel with anyone's terminology at this point. But biblically we should not think of a church as a group with one or two ministers, but rather as a group in which *every one* is a minister.

Notice also from the same biblical passage what the purpose of the ministry is: "for the edifying of the body of Christ" (Eph. 4:12). Edifying means building up. The church is built up in quality and in quantity. I see this saying that pastors should lead and people should minister so that the church grows.

This biblical teaching is found in the middle of a key passage on spiritual gifts. I do not think there is any dimension of the Christian life that more effectively joins the teachings of Scripture with the day-to-day activities of the people of God than spiritual gifts. It is with their spiritual gifts that Christian people minister. Therefore, if a pastor is leading a church to growth one of the essential goals of that leadership is to make sure every member of the church discovers, develops, and is using his or her spiritual gift or gifts.

While the church is subject to many principles of human organizational management, it is much more than a mere human organization. It is the Body of Christ. It is an organism with Jesus Christ as the Head and every member functioning with one or more spiritual gifts. God does not bring people into the Body of Christ as spectators. He expects them to participate in the life and work of the church just as the various members of our own physical bodies contribute to the well-being of the whole.

It is not up to you as a Christian to place an order for the gift or gifts which you might want. God, by His grace and in His wisdom, decides which member of the Body each of us is and He gives us the gifts we need accordingly. Thus, our first responsibility is to discover our gifts. Resources to help do this are becoming more and more available as leaders awaken to the value of laypeople in their churches discovering their gifts. Many denominations now have gifts-discovery materials which are designed to be compatible with the philosophy of ministry of the particular denomination. There are also many nondenominational resources. I feel so strongly about this that I have given a large part of my own ministry to developing resources to help you discover, develop, and use your spiritual gifts. One is a book entitled *Your Spiritual Gifts Can Help Your Church Grow*

(Regal Books). Hardly a week goes by that I don't get a letter from someone telling me how much the book has helped free them for meaningful ministry in the church. I have also designed a six-hour spiritual gifts workshop that any pastor or even layperson with the gift of teaching can use to help a group discover their gifts. It uses the 125-question Modified Houts Questionnaire which helps you see where God might have gifted you on the basis of your past experience. These resources are available from the Charles E. Fuller Institute of Evangelism and Church Growth, Department 352.230, P.O. Box 91990, Pasadena, California 91109-1990.

In many cases just helping people discover, develop and use their spiritual gifts has made the difference between nongrowth and growth in a church. This is not always the case, I would hasten to say. Church growth is complex and there are always many factors that need to work together for growth. Spiritual gifts teaching is not some patent medicine for sick churches, although it can be very useful for most. But it does help in a great many.

In order to see the dynamics of ministry roles in the church, consider the diagram in Figure 2.

On the left of the spectrum the pastor is the minister. This means that the pastor is expected to do just about everything that happens in the church except sit in the pews during the worship service. The pastor is the one who is supposed to lead people to Christ, to counsel the believers who have problems, to visit the sick in the hospital and at home, to monitor the spiritual life of each believer, to say grace at church suppers, to publish the bulletin and the newsletter, to pay the bills, to make a pastoral call to each home every

PASTORAL MINISTRY ROLES

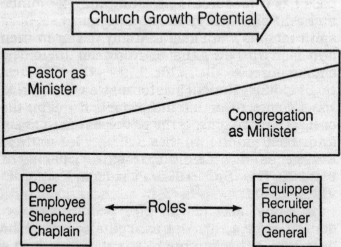

Church Growth Potential

Pastor as
Minister

Congregation
as Minister

Doer
Employee
Shepherd
Chaplain

←———Roles———→

Equipper
Recruiter
Rancher
General

Figure 2

year, to write letters to visitors, to raise the
budget, to keep in touch with college students and
military personnel, to distribute food to the needy
at Christmas time, as well as to preach forty-eight
sermons a year. When a church is far to the left,
failure in any one of these duties is sure to arouse
the comment, "Well, what are we paying the pastor
for, anyhow?"

The church growth potential at the left, where
the pastor is expected to do the ministry of the
church, is exceedingly low around and past the
200 barrier. It can work in small churches, but the
church will find it has a low ceiling on growth.

Growth potential increases as you move to the
right where the pastor actually does less and less
of the ministry of the church. This does not mean
the ministry is neglected. It means that the people

in the congregation decide to become ministers through the use of their spiritual gifts. As the people discover their gifts of teaching and exhortation and service and mercy and healing and evangelism and hospitality and liberality and administration and many others, the Body comes alive. The church grows.

By saying that the pastor ministers less and less, I do not mean that the pastor is not using his or her spiritual gifts. If the pastor has the gifts of faith and leadership, they will be used to their utmost. Usually the gift of teaching will also be there and the pastor will be more of an "equipper" for ministry than a "doer" of ministry, as is indicated in the boxes on the diagram. Rather than being perceived by the congregation as their "employee" to do their work, the pastor is seen as a "recruiter" of others to do what needs to be done in the church. And, as I pointed out in an earlier chapter, as the church grows particularly through the 200 barrier, the pastor must function more and more as a "rancher" and less and less as a "shepherd." To use a military analogy, on the left the pastor serves as "chaplain." That is, he or she cares for the religious needs such as baptism, marriage, burial, and public speaking, but has no leadership role. On the right, however, the pastor is the "general," the officer out in front.

The Pastor and the People in Balance

It is time now to coordinate what was discussed in the last chapter, stressing the pastor as leader and equipper, and what has been stressed in this chapter, namely the laypeople as followers and ministers.

Seeing the two diagrams together gives us a perspective on the whole. In Figure 3 the growth

PASTORAL LEADERSHIP ROLES

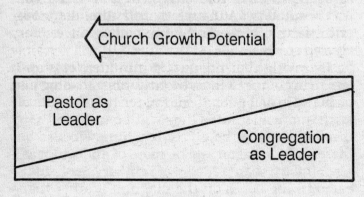

Church Growth Potential

Pastor as
Leader

Congregation
as Leader

Figure 3

PASTORAL MINISTRY ROLES

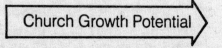

Church Growth Potential

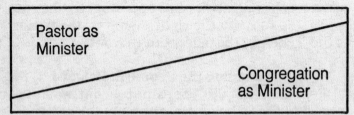

Pastor as
Minister

Congregation
as Minister

Figure 4

potential arrow goes left, toward the pastor. In Figure 4 it goes right, toward the congregation. The pastor's major role for growth is to lead. The congregation's major role for growth is to do the work of the ministry. Although maintaining the proper relationship between the two will not solve every growth problem for every church, it will certainly help unlock tremendous opportunities for growth in many churches presently bogged down in unwieldy pastor-congregation relationships.

Notes

1. Michael Griffiths, *The Church and World Mission* (Grand Rapids: Zondervan Publishing House, 1982), p. 63.

2. John R. Bisagno, *How to Build an Evangelistic Church* (Nashville: Broadman Press, 1971), p. 19.

3. Phillip Keller. *A Shepherd Looks at Psalm 23* (Grand Rapids: Zondervan Publishing House, 1970), pp. 20-21.

4. *Ibid.*, p. 17.

5. "The Changing Focus of Church Finances," interview with Lyle E. Schaller, *Leadership*, Spring, 1981, pp. 14-15.

6. Leon Morris, *The First and Second Epistles to the Thessalonians* (Grand Rapids: Wm. B. Eerdmans Publishing Co., 1959), p. 167.

7. Paul Yonggi Cho, *Successful Home Cell Groups* (Plainfield, NJ: Logos International, 1981), p. 94.

8. Elmer L. Towns, *America's Fastest Growing Churches* (Nashville: Impact Books, 1972), p. 215.

9. *Ibid.*

10. *Ibid.*

11. "A Biblical Style of Leadership?" debate between Larry Richards and Gene Getz, *Leadership*, Spring, 1981, pp. 72-74.

12. Michael Harper, *Let My People Grow: Ministry and Leadership in the Church* (Plainfield, NJ: Logos International, 1977), p. 212.

13. "A Biblical Style of Leadership," p. 77.

14. D. Dewayne Davenport, *The Bible Says Grow: Church Growth Guidelines for Church of Christ* (Williamstown, WV: Church Growth/Evangelism Seminar, 1978), p. 33.

15. *Ibid.* p. 34.

16. *Ibid.*

17. Lyle E. Schaller, *The Multiple Staff and the Larger Church* (Nashville: Abingdon Press, 1980), p. 27.

18. Martin Goldsmith, *Can My Church Grow?* (London: Hodder & Stoughton, 1980), pp. 55-56.

19. John Jennings Merwin, "The Oriental Missionary Society Holiness Church in Japan 1901-1983" (Ph.D. dissertation, Fuller Seminary School of World Mission, Pasadena, Calif., 1983), p. 543.

20. K. Lavern Snider, *It's Happening in Japan Today: The Story of 8 Growing Churches* (Osaka: Japan Free Methodist Mission, 1980), p. 141.

21. Allen L. Swanson, *I Will Build My Church: Ten Case Studies of Church Growth in Taiwan* (Taiwan: Taiwan Church Growth Society, 1977), p. 12.

22. Clarence Lim, "Leadership Development and Church Growth" (unpublished paper, 1982), p. 28.

23. Mardoqueo Munoz, "Senales y Maravillas in la Vida e Historia del Presbiterio Central . . . " (unpublished paper, 1983), p. 14.

24. Gordon Moyes, *How to Grow an Australian Church*, 2nd ed. (Australia: Vital Publications, 1978), p. 45.

25. Floyd Massey and Samuel Berry McKinney, *Church Administration in the Black Perspective* (Valley Forge: Judson Press, 1976), p. 35.

26. Lyle E. Schaller, "Measuring Resistance and Receptivity to Church Growth," *Church Growth: America*, May-June 1981, pp. 4-8.

27. These films are available from the Institute for American Church Growth, 709 E. Colorado Blvd., Suite 150, Pasadena, CA 91101.
28. Charles Mylander, *Secrets for Growing Churches* (San Francisco: Harper & Row Publishers, 1979), p. 2.
29. *Ibid.*, pp. 7-25.

5

Why Bill Bright Is Not Your Pastor

An important clue to church leadership styles can be found in analyzing some of the essential differences between church and parachurch organizations. Unfortunately these essential differences are not well-known because they have not been discussed very frequently either in the literature of pastoral theology or in the seminary classroom.

I am using the terms *church* and *parachurch* loosely. As I will explain, I do not like them very much because I think that both structures are part of the *church* in the broad sense of the word. To imply by the terminology that one structure is really church while the other is something other than church is, to me, focusing the difference between the two on a nonessential quality. The essential differences are something else. But I use the words out of capitulation to the overwhelming popular and current usage.

Modalities and Sodalities

A few years ago my good friend Ralph D. Winter, now director of the U.S. Center for World Mission in Pasadena, California, came up with a set of terms that allow us to be much more precise than church and parachurch, namely *modality* and *sodality*. Some have suggested that because modality and sodality are such esoteric words, it is better to call them *congregational structures* and *missionary structures*. Either way (and I will use both sets of terms), when we begin to understand the fundamental differences between modalities and the leadership they demand on the one hand and sodalities and the leadership they demand on the other, we will also understand one more reason why some of the world's large, growing churches are able to grow the way they do.

The words themselves were taken from different sources. *Modality* is in the dictionary, but is used in the fields of anthropology, music, logic, and medicine. It is not related traditionally to religion. But Winter, an anthropologist by training, adapted the word to refer to what we know as a congregational structure. *Sodality* is also in the dictionary as meaning an association or society such as a Roman Catholic order, and this is the way I am using it here. A sodality is a mission structure.

It is helpful first of all to think of what the modality and sodality structures look like in the secular world.

The modality in the secular world is the city or the municipal structure. It could also be the county or the state or the nation or even the United Nations, but the city is closer to home and easier to understand. The essential nature of the city is that it is a *people-oriented structure*. Members of the city are born into it, they do not have to apply to join. When people move into the city and take up residence, they are automatically members, and they get a vote in the affairs of the city. The obligations for maintaining membership are very few. I recall a recent election of Los Angeles City Council members in which only 15 percent of the registered voters participated. The vast majority did not exercise even the minimal obligation of being a member of the city, but they were not punished for it. Discipline is relatively low—few go to jail, relatively speaking. The basic purpose of the structure is to keep the people in it happy by promoting peace, harmony, and justice. The method is consensus taking. The politician who becomes the mayor is a person who knows what the people want and does his or her best to see that they get it. The ideal is a government "of the people."

Now the sodality structure in the secular world is significantly different. The sodality is not people-oriented, but rather it is a *task-oriented structure.* People do not automatically become members of sodalities, they have to join. They must make some kind of an adult decision and choose to apply to become a member. Examples in the city would include grocery stores, factories, hospitals, theaters, restaurants, and the Rotary Club, all of which are independent of the modality. Others are franchised by the modality such as public utilities, cable TV, and public transportation. Still others are commissioned by the modality such as the police force or the fire department. Notice that in all of these sodality structures the organization is more important than the people. The people who belong to a sodality can be fired if they do not contribute to the purpose of the organization. Many who are fired are very nice persons and upstanding citizens of the modality. But that is a secondary consideration. If they do not help the task, they go. They leave the sodality but not the modality, because the modality is people-oriented, not task-oriented. Obligations in the sodality are many and the discipline is high. The leaders exercise strict accountability and competence of the members is measured and monitored. The leadership cares much less about the consensus of the opinions of the members than about accomplishing the task for which the organization was established.

Congregations and Missions

When we carry these concepts over into the church context, we find a similar pair of structures. The congregational structure, or modality, is the local parish, the district, the diocese, the presbytery, the conference, or the denomination. Notice that the idea of congregational structure includes both the local congregation as well as a cluster of congregations. As in the secular modality, the essential character of the congregational structure is that it is *people-oriented*. New members are socialized into the group. If their parents are members, a well-defined process of incorporating the children has been developed. They are dedicated or baptized as infants and then baptized or confirmed as adolescents. Whichever process is chosen, it is usually designed to make the pathway as broad and easy as possible, because that is the best way to keep the parents content. Those who are members of another congregation can transfer in with a minimum of difficulty.

Consensus taking is considered the best form of leadership in the modality because the people are all-important. In fact, the people can fire the pastor if they feel disgruntled enough to do it. Discipline is low, just as it is in the city. Excommunication is even rarer than people going to jail. There are few obligations for maintaining membership. In some congregational structures members are retained even though they don't attend worship regularly or make significant financial contributions. Southern Baptists, for example, are notorious for retaining members who don't even live in the community where the church is located (about 30 percent of their membership is nonresident).

The mission structure, or sodality, is something else. Its essential nature is a *task-oriented structure.* No one is born into it. All members have to apply to be accepted. It requires a second Christian decision, the first being deciding to become part of the modality by accepting Christ. Competence is required for acceptance. My wife and I, for example, were accepted into two mission structures, in our case foreign mission agencies. Each one of them required a complete medical history as a part of our application. We have also joined six different local churches through the years. Not one of them asked for a medical history! There is room for the lame, the halt, and the blind in the Kingdom of God—but in modalities, not in sodalities. If members of the sodality cannot contribute to the task physically, mentally, or spiritually, they cannot be a part of it. People are important but not so important as the task. Their performance is monitored. Nominality is not tolerated. A high level of commitment is sustained.

Examples of mission structures include Campus Crusade for Christ, Wycliffe Bible Translators, World Vision International, and the American Bible Society to name a few which are independent of the congregational structures. Others, however, are dependent to one degree or another on the congregational structures such as Roman Catholic orders, denominational mission boards, the Evangelism Explosion team in a local church, and the Christian school next to a local church.

The differences between modalities and sodalities are now clear. But here is an interesting point and one which has far-reaching effects on our ideas of church leadership. Let me put it in the words of Richard Hutcheson, who is one of the very few writers in the field who has described it. Hutcheson says, "There is a sense in which the local church itself . . . may be called a 'sodality.' "[1] Many legitimate congregational structures are so ordered that they behave and operate as if they were mission structures, and this has a distinct influence on their growth. A decisive question for the pastor and the people of a church to raise among themselves is: are we willing to allow our church to take on the characteristics of a sodality? Not all are, as we shall see.

The Modality-Sodality Debate

It is one thing to recognize the nature of the sodality or mission structure, but it is another to decide whether it is legitimate. Ralph D. Winter thinks it is, but George W. Peters disagrees. Examining the points of view of these two prominent missiologists will help clarify the issues.

George Peters describes the history of the church in missions as the history of great personalities and missionary societies. He laments that "only in exceptional cases has it been the church in missions." He calls this an "unfortunate and abnormal historic development which has produced autonomous, missionless churches on the one hand and autonomous churchless missionary societies on the other hand."² In Peters's opinion, the causes of this problem are rooted in the theology of the Reformation which did not develop a strong missiology, the failure of the reformers to develop a church independent from the state (Peters himself is a Mennonite and one can see how an Anabaptist would hold this view), and the lack of readiness on the part of the church of the Reformation, being at a low spiritual level, to launch out in missions. Some reformers also, he argues, taught that missions were the obligation of individuals rather than of the church as a whole. All this created a climate so that when strong personalities such as Hudson Taylor and Roland Bingham received their missionary calls, they were forced to move outside the church and form new missionary societies independent of the existing church.

Ralph Winter does not agree that sodalities are either unfortunate or abnormal. He sees both modalities and sodalities as "two structures of God's redemptive mission," which is the title of his landmark essay which uncovered the whole issue a few years ago.³ In it he describes how each of the two structures has existed since biblical times.

The modality was the New Testament church. We find no explicit instructions in the New Testament as to how to organize a New Testament church, Winter argues, because the Jewish believers never gave up the synagogue structure. The pattern of the synagogue became the pattern of the church with God's implicit blessing. It was so familiar that the biblical writers never thought of explaining it. Winter sees the defining characteristic of this structure as including old and young, male and female, former Jews and non-Jewish Greeks, normal biological families in aggregate.

Being born a Jew was enough to make one a member of the synagogue, given the established rites of initiation such as circumcision of males and perhaps an equivalent of what is now called bar mitzvah. The church continued the same. It is revealing to notice how minimal the requirements are for obtaining and maintaining membership in the New Testament churches. Repentance of sins, confession of Jesus as Lord and Saviour, and water baptism seem to be the admission requirements. But even though Jesus had said, "By their fruits shall you know them," overly rigorous standards were not applied to *maintain* membership.

The church at Corinth is a case in point. The church members, whom Paul called "saints" and "sanctified in Christ Jesus" (1 Cor. 1:2), were embroiled in carnal divisionism, eating sacrificial meat in the idol temples, getting drunk at the Holy Communion, dressing like prostitutes, ignoring the poor and needy, abusing spiritual gifts, and denying the doctrine of the resurrection. Yet Paul, while dealing with the situation in great detail, recommended excommunication for only one—a man living openly with is stepmother. Paul scolded the others but did not suggest that they had forfeited their right to church membership because they practiced such deeds. There are other passages where Paul sets forth high requirements for *leaders*, but not for ordinary members. Back then, as now, excommunication in the congregational structure or modality was rare.

The sodality in New Testament times was the missionary band, according to Ralph Winter. Paul's mission is the clearest example. It began, like the church, by taking over an existing Jewish structure, namely the Jewish proselyting band. Jesus referred to these when He said to the Jewish

Pharisees, "For you travel land and sea to win one proselyte" (Matt. 13:15). Jews were much more evangelistic in the first century than they are today. But this is the reason why the organization of the missionary band is not explained in detail in the New Testament—the same reason why the organization of the church is not explained. It was nothing new, it was simply assumed.

Paul's missionary band, as a sodality, was quite different from the New Testament churches. He maintained high requirements for joining and monitored the work of the members. He could and did fire those who were incompetent, with John Mark being the most obvious case (see Acts 15:36-40). Because it was a task-oriented structure and Mark was not contributing well to the task, out he went. The task was more important than the person. Barnabas soon went too, after it was obvious that he and Paul weren't seeing the issues eye to eye. Disharmony among top leadership is not tolerated in the sodality. Why? It stands in the way of goal accomplishment. Notice that Mark was not excommunicated from the congregational structure because it is people-oriented and not task-oriented.

How the Two Relate

I think Ralph Winter is right. I see both modalities and sodalities as part of God's total plan for the church in mission. However if the mission is to be fulfilled, the two must relate to each other in a dynamic way.

Both should be considered structures which bind together the people of God. They are kingdom structures, and they exist for God's glory. Both, in the true sense of the word, are part of the *church*. That is why I do not like to call them churches and parachurch organizations rather than modalities and sodalities. The word *parachurch* means alongside of the church, but implies that it is not the church itself. I realize that many, like George Peters, will have a problem with this ecclesiology, but if so it should not become an obstacle to understanding the basic leadership principles. Peters himself is a strong supporter of sodality-type mission structures, even though theoretically he wishes they were not necessary.[4]

The main point is that in order to accomplish the mission of the church, sodalities and modalities need each other in a symbiotic relationship. The symbiotic relationship means that each one contributes to the well-being of the other. It is the opposite of a parasitic relationship in which the parasite lives off and ultimately destroys the host. Unfortunately sodalities are perceived by some as being parasites, and perhaps there are those who do tend to be that way. But those are the abuses and excesses. The whole relationship should not be rejected just because of occasional bad experiences.

The major contribution of the congregational structure or modality is to provide the *broad vision.* Like the mayor of the city, the pastor needs to see the whole picture and to make sure the pieces all fit together. If there is a need for new restaurants, the mayor of the city does not start them personally, but makes sure that the proper conditions are created so they get started. Likewise the pastor should make sure that sodalities get started in order to accomplish certain tasks. The congregation needs to provide resources such as prayer, personnel, finances, and moral support. Sodalities usually will not start other sodalities, so the modality with its broad vision needs to see that it is done.

Pastors of large, growing churches should not try to do everything any more than the mayor of the city could. They should delegate responsibility for accomplishing tasks to those who have the specialized know-how to do them. I know of no church which provides more services to its surrounding community than the Crystal Cathedral in Garden Grove, California. They can do it because pastor Robert Schuller understands the sodality principle. He has created conditions for the development of no less than eighty internal mission structures which run satellite ministries from the Hour of Power television program to the Crystal Cathedral Academy; from the New Hope Counseling Services to the Literacy Center; from the Institute for Successful Church Leadership to the Helping Hands which distributes food and clothing to the needy, and on and on.

The modality provides the broad vision, but the sodality is not expected to do this. That would be against its nature. The very nature of a good sodality is its *narrow vision*, its focus on a specific task. Richard Hutcheson explains that "they generally start from scratch and focus on one charismatic leader and one cause."[5] Because of its task-orientation and its inherent narrow vision, the leader of a well-functioning sodality will usually be characterized by three peculiar attitudes:

First, they think their task is the most important task in the Kingdom of God. They respect what others are doing, but they have experienced such an urgency to their call that they cannot imagine any other ministry as important as theirs. That is why they can go at what they are doing with a passion which far surpasses that of the ordinary leader of the congregational structure or modality.

Second, they believe that they are the only ones doing the particular task well. Few say this in public because it would appear altogether immodest. They treat leaders of similar sodalities with great respect and refer to their works with careful diplomacy. But if they are good sodality leaders they believe in their hearts that their particular methodology is superior to others, and if they doubt for a moment that it might not be superior, they will take immediate steps to rectify the situation.

The two above attitudes, which are precisely what are necessary for excellence in performing the task, often get good sodality leaders in trouble. They tend to irritate the modality leaders and also other sodality leaders. To the degree they don't, they are usually less effective. But the modality leaders should not allow themselves to be irritated by this because they should maintain the broad vision and be the ones to see that such attitudes on the part of sodality leaders are ultimately helpful to the Kingdom of God.

The third attitude characteristic of good sodality leaders is a relatively low need for people. By this I mean that personally and psychologically they do not crave deep, long-term, heart-to-heart relationships with persons outside their immediate family. They know either consciously or subconsciously that to the degree they become personally involved with others they may lose the objectivity required to monitor their performance in accomplishing the task. It is always a temptation to get their eyes off the task and on people. This does not prevent some of them from spending the time with a few middle-management leaders and pouring their lives into them in a discipling relationship. But they do this only as they see that it facilitates the task.

Now you may begin to see why Bill Bright, a sodality leader par excellence, is not your pastor. If he were a pastoral type leader, Campus Crusade for Christ wouldn't be what it is today.

If you check it out, you will find that usually the first generation founding leaders of a sodality will score high on the three attitudes above. But the second and third generation leaders will score lower. How does the charismatic leader make provision for an equally charismatic replacement? Usually, as Max Weber explained decades ago, it is impossible. But I want to deal with this important subject in more detail in another chapter.

An Historical Clarification

We saw how modalities and sodalities can be traced back to New Testament times. But a brief look at subsequent history can also be helpful to understand their dynamics. Some of the most effective mission structures in Christian history were the monasteries. When you think of it, from the fall of the Roman Empire until well after the Reformation of the sixteenth century, God's premier instrument for carrying the gospel throughout the earth was the monsateries. This is thoroughly documented in the many works of historian Kenneth Scott Latourette who understood the modality-sodality dynamic very well. Ralph Winter has also elaborated on this in considerable detail.

Sadly, world evangelization was not a prominent activity of the Protestant reformers or the churches they started. We looked at some reasons given by George Peters for this. However there may be another reason even more significant. Martin Luther, who as an Augustinian monk was the member of a sodality, turned so radically against the Roman Catholic church that he threw out the baby with the bathwater. He got rid of the Catholic orders but did not replace them with similar Protestant sodalities. Lutheran historian Jarislav Pelikan affirms that Luther was not able to come up with "a proposal to replace the structure of the missionary orders, whose monastic rules Luther had repudiated, with some other structure that would carry on the missionary imperative . . . A century and a half were to pass before his followers could begin to produce such a structure."[6] The Christian movement was still expanding during those 150 years, but mostly by the Roman Catholics and their sodalities. Luther's sound theology was not sound missiology.

The Anabaptists were also spreading the gospel, particularly among nominal Christians, in the sixteenth century. They never lost the missionary zeal. The Great Commission is prominent in Anabaptist writings. But notice that the nature of the Anabaptist movement was a sodality-type structure. While it was a church, it required a second adult decision to join. Infant baptism, whether by Catholics or Lutherans or Reformed, was rejected. All members had to be baptized or rebaptized as adults, and by immersion. Life-style requirements were strictly enforced. Nominality was not tolerated, even on the part of children of believers. Excommunication was practiced. The church grew tremendously even amidst persecution.

As a result of their essential differences, modalities historically have a difficult time coexisting with sodalities. The tendency is for modalities to consume sodalities, or for sodalities to gradually become more and more like modalities in their structure and attitudes.

The Anabaptists are a case in point. Examine the Anabaptist movement now, with all its branches, and you will see a cluster of modalities. Some are so sealed off and so highly endogamous that converts from the outside are excluded almost by definition. Others have so identified with the mainstream of Christianity that the zeal of the founders has become nostalgia. Some, such as the Mennonite Brethren, have created new mission structures which recapture some of the original sodality zeal that the entire church once had. When old sodalities weaken or disappear, new ones must be formed to take their place.

Another case is the Methodists. John Wesley, the founder, was an Anglican priest who had no idea of beginning a denomination that would compete with the Anglicans. He preached the gospel and gathered his converts, all presumably Anglicans, into "classes" which were small sodalities. But after Wesley's death, the Anglican church could not cope with the phenomenon and the classes congealed into a new denomination which itself functioned in the beginning like a sodality. However, a couple of centuries later, the United Methodist church is a classic modality structure. The sodalities have been consumed.

Social scientists, following Ernst Troeltsch, call the original sodality a "sect" and the resulting modality a "church." The church-sect typology has been a chief focal point of research into sociology of religion, and the historical tendencies described above have been amply confirmed. Sects almost invariably become churches over a period of time.

A number of observers, for example, have noticed that the fundamentalist movement of the early twentieth century had the characteristics of a sect, but now the evangelical movement which grew from it has many characteristics of a church. Some fundamentalists have recently also been moving away from their sect ethos, much to the consternation of the old guard. The classic Pentecostal denominations began as sects, but now in their quest for respectability are also becoming more like churches.

All this would be a historic curiosity except that there is a clear bearing on the growth of churches. As the sect becomes a church or as the sodality becomes a modality the level of commitment and zeal goes lower and lower. As this happens, the church growth dynamic decreases, and we need to examine this phenomenon in some detail.

Church Structures and Growth Potential

Most local churches are classic modalities. They are organized like modalities and they are led like modalities. The pastors are people-oriented and they run their church by consensus. For the most part this is what they were trained to do in seminary, and this is what both they and the church members feel their pastor is hired to do in the particular church. Some of these churches are growing, but most of them are not growing well.

As I have studied growing churches around the world, I have experienced an increasing awareness which at first puzzled me. I had assumed that all local churches were modalities by definition. But then I began to realize that many of the leadership characteristics of the pastors of the large, growing local churches were strikingly similar to those of successful sodality leaders. It then began to dawn on me that it is possible for a local church to be a great deal like a sodality, and that to the degree it tends that way it enjoys a higher growth potential. It seems that the more pastors can lead their churches like sodalities instead of modalities, the more growth they can expect.

This must be explained because it could arouse a great deal of misunderstanding. Let me begin by looking at Figure 5.

Church Growth Potential

Congregational structure
Pastor as modality leader

Mission structure
Pastor as sodality leader

Church	Sect/parachurch
Pluralistic	Like-minded
Stresses being	Stresses doing
People-oriented	Task-oriented
Government by consensus	Government by vision
Maintenance-oriented	Mission-oriented
Biological growth	Second-decision growth
Lower commitment	Higher commitment

Figure 5

The first thing I want to point out is that we have here a spectrum. We are not talking about *either* a congregational structure *or* a mission structure. We are suggesting a trend toward one or the other in eight different areas. As you match your church to the eight categories you will probably lean toward one direction on one and another on the other. But the profile will allow you to see how many sodality characteristics you may now have or you may want in the future. The helpful thing about it is that it allows you to raise some questions about your church which otherwise might not surface.

For instance, do you see yourselves as a *church* or a *sect* as we have been discussing them? Are you pretty well conformed to the culture around you so that you are considered "respectable," or are you measurably different from the secular people you know? Are you *pluralistic,* allowing a wide diversity of people with many different points of view in your church, or are you pretty much *like-minded* and strict on your doctrine and practice? If you are pluralistic you are probably more liberal than your like-minded or conservative neighbors. Do you think that *being* is more important than *doing?* Is the way you play the game more important than whether you win or lose? If it is, you are probably also more *people-oriented* than *task-oriented.*

How about the way your church is led? Do you find that major changes come about mostly through a general *consensus* of the active members or through the *vision* of the pastor? Do you insist on a long, drawn-out planning process or are you accustomed to rather abrupt changes in direction? Are you *maintenance-oriented* or *mission-oriented?* Is most of your ministry and activity focused on those already in the church or do you regularly and effectively minister to those outside? Do most of your new members come through socializing the children of existing members or do you draw heavily form the surrounding pool of unchurched? The former is called *biological growth* and the latter *second-decision growth.* Where would you place your church members on a scale running from *lower commitment* to *higher commitment?*

I imagine that most churches that wrestle with these questions will find themselves pretty much on the left, or modality, side of the spectrum. To the degree that this is the case, however, your growth potential will be lower. To the degree you find yourselves on the right, or sodality side, or to the degree you are willing to move in that direction, growth potential rises. In order to move in that direction you will need to look at at least two very important qualities of growing churches: sodality-type leadership and sodality-type commitment. Let's discuss them one at a time.

Sodality-type Leadership

In chapter 1 I mentioned that several computer tests have been made on the vital signs of a healthy church as found in the book *Your Church Can Grow*. One of these was done by William R. Douglass at Seattle University. The vital sign which correlated most with church growth was the one on strong leadership. Douglass found that the pastor of a growing church "needs to be high on task orientation and low on relationship orientation. In other words, an achiever."[7] This is a description of a sodality-type leader. But it raises an important question: how can you lead a church effectively and at the same time be low on relationship orientation? Is not the relationship between the pastor and the people an essential ingredient to the effective leadership in a local church? Obviously, yes. How to focus on the task and yet maintain vital relationships is the issue.

As a basis for discussion, I would like to use a very helpful diagram produced by a student of mine, missionary Raymur Downey of Zaire. Downey sees two axes as crucial to church growth leadership and relates them to each other (see Fig. 6).

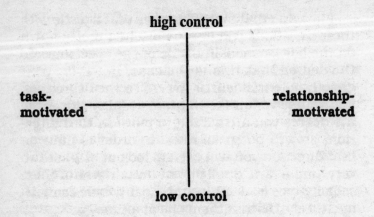

Figure 6

Look first at the horizontal axis between task-motivation and relationship-motivation. Obviously the task side best describes our sodality leader. This means that the leader is motivated to assume a position of leadership primarily because he or she sees a significant task which needs to be done. It does not mean that the task-motivated leader is oblivious of the need for good personal relationships. It does not reflect a lack of love for others. Many task-motivated leaders have exceedingly good track records of recruiting peers for leadership positions and recruiting members who become followers. Many sodality-type pastors whom I know have fiercely loyal staffs of highly competent leaders. They will tell you how much their senior pastor has poured his or her life into them and helped them to become what they are. Relationships are excellent, but they are not the starting point. The staff members I just mentioned also know that the moment they cease making their contribution to the task, they are out. They will be fired in love.

Now look at the vertical axis from high control to low control. This refers to the amount of authority which is invested in the senior pastor. Remember what we said in the last chapter about the pastor-sheep relationship? The person at the high control point is functioning as a pastor who guides the sheep. The pastor is the leader and the people follow. But recall also how this is attained. It must be earned by proving to the people that you, the pastor, are their servant. The more the people gain confidence that their pastor truly is their servant, the more you slide up on the control scale. The higher you go, the more of a sodality-type leader you are.

Very few pastors will be totally task-motivated and in total control of the situation. But the further you move toward the upper left side of the diagram, the more you lead the church like a sodality-type leader. The more you find yourself toward the lower right hand side the more of a modality-type leader you are. The church growth potential, needless to say, is higher in the upper left quadrant: task-motivated and high pastoral control.

Sodality-type Commitment

If you have been testing your own local church against the modality-sodality diagram and would like to see it become more like a sodality, you need to look not only at leadership, but also at commitment: One of the chief characteristics of sodalities as we have been describing them is a high level of dedication on the part of its members. Nominality is not tolerated. Discipline is strict. "Shape up or ship out!" is the motto.

The religious world is deeply indebted to Dean M. Kelley of the National Council of Churches for his landmark volume *Why Conservative*

Churches Are Growing, published in the early 1970s. In it Kelley demonstrates convincingly that the stricter the church, the stronger it is, and the higher the growth potential. Kelley's stronger churches are characterized by high degrees of commitment, discipline, and missionary zeal. There is strong group solidarity and heavy demands are made on the members. The charismatic leader is obeyed without much question. You will find high levels of absolutism, conformity, and fanaticism. There is little tolerance of deviance or dissent. This is what I call sodality-type commitment.

If you are interested in moving your church toward a stronger sodality-type of commitment level, I suggest you go about it in two ways:

First, raise your requirements for new members. If it is easy to become a member of your church now, make it more difficult. If you have no new members' class, start one. If you have one, consider making it longer and more demanding. Many very successful new members' classes run up to ten weeks. The content of these classes will depend on your philosophy of ministry, which I will discuss in the next chapter. Do not allow anyone, no matter who, to be an exception to the rule. I can well remember the day I made application to join Lake Avenue Congregational Church. I was a mature Christian, an ordained minister, a veteran missionary, the executive of a missionary agency, and a theological seminary professor. I also had a very tight schedule on weekends, and the requirements for membership were to attend a series of six consecutive Sunday new members' classes. I explained my situation to the pastor, hoping that I would be considered an exception to the rule. I was told very politely, but firmly, that I was welcome to attend the church but would have to rearrange my schedule and take those classes if I wanted to join. What did I do? I rearranged my schedule. And I have been highly impressed ever since at my church's strength. Without it it couldn't have grown to an attendance of around 3,000 in an area of population decline.

Second, raise the commitment level for the current members. There are many ways to do this, but one of the best is currently being used by my good friend Larry DeWitt, pastor of Calvary Community of Thousand Oaks, California. In the past six years Calvary Community has grown from less than 20 to an attendance of over 2,000. They meet in a leased warehouse, but have the property and the plans for a sanctuary seating 2,500. They have always been a sodality-type commitment church, but now they are stricter. DeWitt recently introduced the "Oaks of Righteousness" plan. An artist created a large oak tree on the wall of the church with places for 1,000 signatures. The requirements for becoming an oak of righteousness are as high as I have seen in a church. You must sign your name to a covenant, making a commitment to six minimum weekly requirements:

1. Attendance at weekly worship.
2. Spending one night per week with the family in planned family activities.
3. Participating in a small growth group which meets weekly.
4. Committing yourself to regular, substantial giving to the church.
5. Locating a ministry in the church in which you can use your spiritual gifts.
6. Promising to spend time each day in personal devotions.

Over half of those who are active in the life of

Calvary Community have put their names on the oak tree, and more are making the commitment all the time. No wonder the church is growing and sustaining its growth.

Leading your church to growth means that as much as circumstances will permit, you should attempt to lead your church like a sodality.

Notes

1. Richard G. Hutcheson, Jr., *Wheel Within the Wheel: Confronting the Management Crisis of the Pluralistic Church* (Atlanta: John Knox Press, 1979), p. 113.

2. G. W. Peters, *A Biblical Theology of Missions* (Chicago: Moody Press, 1972), p. 214.

3. Ralph D. Winter, "The Two Structures of God's Redemptive Mission," *Missiology: An International Review*, January 1974, pp. 121-139.

4. See George W. Peters, *A Theology of Church Growth* (Grand Rapids: Zondervan Publishing Co., 1981), pp. 172-183.

5. Richard G. Hutcheson, Jr., *Mainline Churches and the Evangelicals: A Challenging Crisis?* (Atlanta: John Knox Press, 1981), p. 161.

6. Jarislav Pelikan, *Spirit Versus Structure: Luther and the Institutions of the Church* (New York: Christian Classics, 1968), pp. 55-56.

7. William R. Douglass, "Identifying Variables Associated with Church Growth through Regression Analysis" (research paper, Seattle University, 1978), p. 67.

8. Dean M. Kelley, *Why Conservative Churches are Growing* (New York: Harper & Row Publishers, 1972), p. 84.

6

Getting the Right Start

Are you ready to grow? If you are convinced that God wills the growth of His church, if you are willing to pay the price for growth, if the pastor is prepared to assume the responsibility for growth leadership, and if the congregation has decided to follow that growth leadership, you may well be ready.

If so, how do you go about it? This chapter will offer a few practical suggestions for starting a growth process in your church. The next chapter will list a few more suggestions on how to keep going once you've started. They don't say everything which needs to be said. You will find much more in the growing body of church growth literature. But I have selected what I consider to be the priority steps toward a successful start toward growth.

Calling the Right Pastor

If all I have said in the previous chapters is

valid, the starting point for leading your church to growth must be the right pastor. The growth potential for many churches, unfortunately, is very low because the current pastor either does not have a vision for growth or is not willing to pay the price. Where this is the case, either the pastor must change his or her attitude toward growth or the pastor himself must be changed. Pastors' attitudes can be changed. I know because I have witnessed it numerous times in my classes and seminars. If the pastor wants to change, abundant resources are available which can help, as I have previously mentioned. But if such resources are not welcomed, it may be time to start thinking about a new pastor.

Pray for the right person

The first step in finding the right pastor is prayer. One bedrock assumption of Christian ministry is that a pastor serves a given church in directed response to the call of God. Many pastors are misfits because somehow they have missed their call and are not in the church where God wants them. This is why prayer is essential. All concerned—whether the congregation, the pulpit committee, the candidate, or the denominational authorities—need to be so sensitive to hearing the voice of God in the matter that the chances of missing the call will be low. I know of no other way to attain this sensitivity than through a large quantity of high quality prayer. This means setting aside significant time for prayer, which is not easy for most action-oriented Americans to do. Our tendency is to get the prayer over with as soon as possible so we can get down to the "real business." But unless we consider prayer "real business" we run high risks of inviting a pastor whom

God may want elsewhere.

Look for the qualities you need

The second step is to begin to look for a person with the qualities which you feel you need. A common pitfall of pulpit committees is to draw up a list of all the ideal qualities they would like to see in a pastor and look for someone who scores high on all. They list everything short of walking on water. The apostle Paul himself would not qualify in many cases. Making the list of qualities too long is usually frustrating and excessively time-consuming.

Each congregation will clearly have certain priority qualities that they feel their pastor must have. In addition to those, I suggest that if you are looking for the kind of pastor who will help the church grow you include at least the following six qualities. I would not expect any candidate to be a "10" in all six, but scoring above average in at least five of the six is a good starting point.

1. *The pastor must be a leader.* Look for a person who is called to be out front. In this book I have attempted to describe the attributes of such a leader in great detail. But don't forget that the acid test of a leader is whether there are followers and that their decision to follow has been voluntary. The best way to find this out is to interview members of churches the candidate has previously served. Another way, recommended in the Bible, is to check out the candidate's relationship with his or her family. If there is a good relationship with the spouse and children and if the individual has proved to be a good family leader you have a green light. "For if a man does not know how to rule his own house, how will he take care of the church of God?" (1 Tim. 3:5).

2. *The pastor must be a person of faith.* Whether it is through a special spiritual gift or whether it comes through development of the fruit of the Spirit, a church growth pastor is characterized by faith. Read about Abraham and Moses and David and the others in Hebrews 11. "But without faith it is impossible to please Him" (Heb. 11:6). A person of faith is focused on tomorrow rather than yesterday. Setting goals comes naturally to such a leader. A pastor with faith has a high degree of assurance that he or she knows in which direction God wants the church to move in the future.

3. *The pastor must be a possibility thinker.* Gloomy pastors subject to depression and defeat are not usually growth pastors. If the candidate is overly critical, a negative thinker, and prone to bring out what is wrong rather than what is right about a given situation you have a yellow light: caution. Possibility thinkers know how to turn problems into opportunities. They usually relate well to others because they themselves have sufficiently high self-esteem. Faith sets the direction, possibility thinking discovers creative ways of getting the job done.

4. *The pastor must be a good preacher.* While I know of few growth pastors who do not handle themselves admirably in the pulpit, I would hasten to say that some pulpit committees overemphasize preaching to the extent that it is virtually the only quality they really look for. Many growth pastors are not golden-mouthed orators, but they understand the function of the pulpit in the broader context of worship, leadership, and group dynamics. Try to make sure that the preacher is receptor-oriented, gearing the ministry to the felt needs of the congregation. Don't confuse communication, which is highly important, with elo-

quence, which is of minimal importance.

5. *The pastor must be flexible.* Church growth means constant change. Pastors who are strongly oriented toward tradition and who are uncomfortable with innovation are not growth pastors. Ask God for a person who knows when to change in the light of fresh challenges. At this point consecrated pragmatism is a desirable quality.

6. *The pastor must be a hard worker.* I have mentioned this before, but I will mention it again. I agree with Lyle Schaller when he says, "Most effective pastors share one common characteristic: each is a remarkably hard worker."[1]

Be sure you all agree

The third step in finding the right pastor is to be sure that all parties concerned are operating from the same assumption base. There must be as high a level of agreement as possible among the members of the pulpit committee, the candidate, and the denominational executive at the beginning of the process. One of the most confusing and disheartening situations arises when, after a great deal of time, effort, and energy is invested in identifying a candidate who looks like the right person, conflicting assumptions rise to the surface. Granted, it is better to have them surface before rather than after a call is extended, but the best of all is to prevent it from happening. I am aware of two good resources currently available to pulpit committees. One is Lyle E. Schaller's book *The Pastor and the People* (Abingdon Press, 1973). The other is a whole kit designed by Gerald M. Williamson which includes the *Pastor Search Committee Primer,* the *Pastor Search Committee Planbook* and a cassette tape (Broadman Press, 1981). This one takes the committee step by step through a very well-worked-out process.

While these resources are fairly exhaustive, I want to stress four questions which are particularly relevant to calling a church growth pastor. They should be clear and up front for all parties involved.

1. *Are we willing to provide adequate compensation?* "You get what you pay for" is not supposed to be true in the Lord's service. Although it is clearly less true in Christian work than in secular work, nevertheless it should not be ignored. More pastors than we would like to believe change churches largely because the new one offers a higher salary, a more comfortable manse, or better fringe benefits. The Bible says that the laborer is worthy of his hire, and pulpit committees should not forget it—because pastors don't. Fairly routine items such as manse allowance or church-owned housing, automobile allowance, insurance of various kinds, retirement accounts, moving expenses, and vacations need to be mutually understood, the sooner the better.

One other relatively uncommon item in the compensation package needs to be stressed. If the congregation and the pastor are both serious about growth and willing to pay the price, part of this price is plugging into the new church growth technology which continues to be developed. The church should make plans to invest an annual amount for on-the-job training for the pastor. One or two weeks a year including whatever budget is necessary for travel, tuition, expenses and pulpit supply is a wise provision for the church to make. Presumably the pastor is being called for an extended period of time, and it is important that the leader be current with what is developing in the field. This should not be considered a fringe benefit or a substitute for vacation. It should be considered part of the job, and an investment in the future of the church.

2. *Will the pastor be allowed to be a rancher?* This is a tough question to raise because it seems at first so contrary to traditional concepts of a pastor. But if the growth goals of your church reach significantly beyond the 200 barrier, it is a necessary one. What does being a rancher imply? A short time ago my good friend Kent Tucker answered that question for me. Tucker is the founding pastor of Grace Church in Aurora, Colorado. Only three years old, it has moved through the 200 barrier relatively smoothly. One reason for this is that Tucker, from the very outset, agreed with his people that he would serve them as a rancher. This meant, among other things, that he would not visit the homes of the members, he would not visit them in the hospital, and that he would not do any one-on-one counseling. Because it is a new church, there was no contrary tradition to change as there would be in most other churches. All new members learn that this is the policy before they decide to join the church.

As a good rancher, however, Tucker has made provision for the care of the sheep by others. He has the congregation divided into several "mini-churches" with an elder that he has trained as the leader of each minichurch. The elder is in charge of visiting the homes, visiting the hospital, and counseling. He can do it himself or delegate it. When a counseling problem arises which needs a pastor's touch, Tucker will see the person, but only if the elder accompanies the one needing help.

3. *How much outside activity may the pastor undertake?* The vision of church growth pastors

frequently extends past the local congregation. A network of relationships is built up which can open wider vistas for ministry. They are often in fairly high demand as speakers and consultants.

In the light of this, how willing is the congregation to share the pastor with others? How much time can be spent out of town? Is the pastor allowed to use ministry time for writing for publication? The assumptions on these questions need to be made clear on both sides in order to prevent future misunderstandings.

4. *Does the pastor match our sociocultural profile?* I cannot count the number of conversations I have had with pastors concerning their first parish assignment. All too frequently a new seminary graduate, born and raised in an urban environment, is invited to serve a small rural congregation. The idealism of the typical seminary student blinds him or her to the crucial role that culture plays in the proper pastor-parish match. The graduate thinks that all churches are the same and says, "I can serve any church whatsoever." Reality is something different, though, and often the first parish assignment is a nightmare for the new pastor. It usually doesn't hurt the church very much, though, because the people are used to seeing pastors like that. There have been many of them before.

While Americans indoctrinated with the melting pot theory of social reality are typically reluctant to talk about differences of regional origin, class, race, education, economic status, ethnicity and the like, these factors are nevertheless highly important in predicting whether a pastor-parish match will succeed. Unusual exceptions to the rule pop up here and there, but generally speaking the growth potential will be higher when the new pastor has a sociocultural orientation similar to that of most members of the congregation.

Write a Philosophy of Ministry

It is much easier to call a pastor if your church has a written philosophy of ministry. This gets the assumptions out in the open where everyone concerned can study and discuss them. It is also a tremendous help for future church growth planning.

The term "philosophy of ministry" is relatively new, but highly useful. It allows us to become conscious of the fact that each church, like each individual person, has a unique personality. No two churches are exactly alike. True, Assemblies of God churches are more like each other than they are like Mennonite churches, but even within the Assemblies of God each church is different. As a matter of fact, there are four large, prestigious Assemblies of God in Springfield, Missouri, the denominational headquarters. All have 500-1000 members and are healthy. But all are different. Central Assembly is a traditional church with a well-ordered service and the prestige which appeals to many denominational executives and professors. Calvary Assembly has been built around evangelistic preachers and features a strong Sunday evening evangelistic service. It has a fairly high age profile. Parkcrest Assembly is a newer church in a housing development area, and is family-centered with a considerable amount of affluence. Evangel Temple, founded in the 1960s by a professor, uses more contemporary styles of worship and music and thus attracts students and young adults. All are fine churches, but different.

Church growth leaders have learned not just to live with diversity, but to rejoice in it. Unbelievers come in such a great variety that the more different kinds of churches there are, the more options they have for finding Jesus Christ.

No church can do everything. No church can meet everyone's needs. No church can minister well to all people. Therefore, choices concerning excellence in ministry must be made. It is a poor approach to say, "We'll fit in a little bit of everything for everybody." Radio stations discovered a long time ago that it is better to specialize. Rock stations don't mix in a little bit of classical music or vice versa. If they did their clientele would go down to practically nothing. It is better to set ministry priorities and do a few things well rather than attempt many things in a mediocre way.

Let me illustrate what I mean by briefly describing four churches in the Los Angeles area, all of which I admire greatly. These four churches, with weekly attendance running from 1,000 to 8,000, are obviously meeting the felt needs of large numbers of people. But their philosophies of ministry are dramatically different.

The *classroom church*[2] centers on teaching the Word of God. Worship is built around a forty-five-to sixty-minute verse-by-verse expository message. Very little time is spent in singing, "worship," announcements, taking offerings, or liturgy. The people do not come so much for that as to learn more about the Bible. They bring a couple of versions of the Bible for comparison, along with thick notebooks. Outlines of the sermon are distributed and the click-clack of notebook rings is part of the usual noise level. The ministry priorities of the classroom church are taken largely from the agenda of believers. One of the prime examples of the classroom church is Grace Community Church of the Valley in Panorama City, California.

On the average Sunday morning 8,000 people from the San Fernando Valley flock to the services to hear Pastor John MacArthur expound the Word.

The *life-situation church* is significantly different. It establishes ministry priorities primarily on the agenda not of believers but of unbelievers. Its upfront ministry is for the unchurched. My example is the Crystal Cathedral of Garden Grove, California, pastored by Robert Schuller. Schuller says he doesn't like to preach, he likes to witness. His sermons are short, topical talks, loaded with personal illustrations. He rarely quotes the Bible because he did a research project some years ago and discovered that unchurched people in Orange County don't believe the Bible. So he directs his sermons to their felt needs such as their family, their job, their financial situation, their self-esteem or their emotions, explaining how Jesus can meet those needs. Architecture is important. The church is made of 10,000 pieces of glass with reflecting pools and fountains not only on the outside, but also up the center aisle of the sanctuary. Music is important, and the church has invested in one of the largest and most spectacular pipe organs, literally, in the world. Special events are important such as a spectacular annual Christmas pageant featuring live animals. Last year 80,000 people paid ten dollars apiece to witness it. Worship attendance at the Crystal Cathedral is also around 8,000.

The *rock generation church* is something else. Its target is the youth of the baby boom, now between 18 and 30 years of age. The example is Vineyard Christian Fellowship of Yorba Linda, California, pastored by my close friend and colleague, John Wimber. Free-flowing worship and praise is a high priority of ministry with a full forty-five minutes of unbroken chorus singing at the beginning of the service. There is no pipe organ, but rather guitars, drums, and a keyboard which Wimber himself plays. The worship sets a mood for an unusually powerful presence of the Holy Spirit who ministers through prophecies, tongues, words of knowledge, healings, signs, wonders, deliverances and dancing in the spirit. Dress is important. Men do not wear neckties and women do not wear skirts—the people dress as if they were attending a rock concert, but there is no rock music. The place is important. Services are held in a high school gymnasium which is much too hot, stuffy, and smelly for the older generation. Home groups, called kinship groups, are important. There the members of the Body minister to one another. In six years Vineyard Christian Fellowship has grown from 17 to 5,000.

The *spiritual high church* has a fourth philosophy of ministry. Its target is believers who, because of their lot in life, need a strong emotional experience on a weekly basis. My example is Paradise Baptist Church, one of the more prominent black churches of Los Angeles, which when I visited it some time ago was pastored by the late Aaron Iverson. Music is important, but it is quite different from the tall-steeple traditions of the Crystal Cathedral or the low-key choruses of Vineyard. It features a strong rhythmic beat, with much clapping and swaying and great emotion. The sermon is central, but it is not designed for cognitive input. No one has a three-ring notebook. People expect feeling and experience from the sermon. There is a dynamic interchange of shouting back and forth between the pulpit and the pew. The noise level is extremely high. Male and female ushers, all in uniforms with white gloves, are on hand to care for those who pass out, overcome with emotion. They are occasionally called upon to carry people out bodily who are kicking and screaming under the power of the Holy Spirit. The church owns a mortuary, meeting a traditional cultural need for burial security, and the mortuary is advertised in full color on the back cover of the ten-page church bulletin. Attendance when I visited was around 1,000.

I have spoken to laypeople from all four of these churches and have discovered a general feeling among them that their particular church is Number One. They believe that their philosophy of ministry is the very best and the most biblical. From my perspective, however, I see all four philosophies of ministry as good and true and pleasing to God. But they are certainly different, and each one is reaching and ministering to different kinds of people.

Your church is probably different from any of the four I have mentioned. Mine is. But just how different is it? What does your church have that other churches in your community don't have? As you work on verbalizing your philosophy of ministry, there are many things you will need to consider. I will name a few of them with the understanding that the list is not exhaustive. Consider your *worship format* with your order of service, your liturgy, the noise level, expected audience response, punctuality, loose or tight structure, spontaneity, and interpersonal relationships such as greeting the visitors. Consider your *musical program* with the style of music, the quantity, the roles of the choir and the congregation, the instruments used. Consider your *preaching style*—whether expository or topical, cognitive or experi-

ence oriented, low-key or emotional, the length of
the sermon, and the invitation, if any. Consider
the *felt needs of the audience* which are frequently specific to the sociocultural situation, the
educational level, and even sometimes the occupational preference of the people. Consider the *leadership style* which I have elaborated upon in other
sections of this book.

Consider your *charismatic or non-charismatic
orientation* with the public or private use of spiritual gifts. Are the charismatics gifts encouraged,
tolerated, or prohibited? Consider your *fellowship
structures* including your policies on home cell
groups, adult Sunday School classes or special
interest groups. Consider the function of the *Sunday School* whether it is for adults or children or
both, for cognitive input or for fellowship. Consider your *evangelistic strategy* and your attitude
toward public invitations, door-to-door visitation,
use of programs available in the denominational
market or the open market. Consider your *attitude toward ethical issues* such as taking political stands, feeding the poor, divorce, abortion,
homosexuality, smoking, drinking, obesity, etc.
Finally, consider your *size*. Part of your philosophy of ministry should be an intelligent seeking of
God's will as to what is the optimum size needed to
carry out effectively the philosophy of ministry you
have established. This will make a substantial difference in your future planning.

Once you have thought through these issues
and others which are important to you, you are
ready to write the philosophy of ministry for your
church. As you do, keep in mind these five characteristics of a dynamic philosophy of ministry:

It is explicit. It must be written down, not just
taken for granted. Writing disciplines thinking,

and as you go through several drafts God will reveal new and creative things to you.

It is mutual. The philosophy of ministry is the same for both the pastor and the people. Many churches get in trouble and cannot grow because the people have one set of expectations, but the pastor is working off a different agenda.

It is a conviction. If you do not believe your philosophy of ministry is the best and the most biblical, you need to work on it some more. You must respect other churches, but I hope you believe in your heart that your church is Number One.

It is stable. Churches that change their philosophy of ministry frequently lose growth potential. If the philosophy of ministry is working, call a pastor who agrees with it ahead of time.

It is open to modification. This characteristic balances the one above. Nothing should be set entirely in concrete. If flaws become evident they should be subject to change. My advice is, keep your philosophy of ministry open to change, but do not change it easily.

Diagnosing the Health of Your Church

As starting points for a growth process in your church I have mentioned *calling the right pastor* and *writing a philosophy of ministry*. My third suggestion is to *diagnose the health of your church.*

The church is often referred to in the Bible as the Body of Christ. A body, as we all know, can be sick or it can be healthy. If it is healthy it is exhibiting most of the seven vital signs which I have listed in my book *Your Church Can Grow* (Regal Books, 1976) and which I have described elsewhere in this book. In most cases a healthy church will be growing. If the church is not healthy and not growing it may be suffering from one of the growth-inhibiting diseases. In another book, *Your Church Can Be Healthy* (Abingdon Press, 1979), I have attempted to identify eight of the major growth-inhibiting diseases. It will be well to review them briefly here.

Ethnikitis is one of the two terminal illnesses on the list. It is the disease caused by a changing community and is the greatest killer of churches in America. It afflicts neighborhood churches which typically draw their membership from the immediate surrounding community. They have grown through the years by ministering to the needs of the people of the neighborhood, but due to circumstances beyond their control, the neighborhood has changed with new kinds of people moving in and the other people moving out. In advanced ethnikitis a large number of church members now commute to the worship service from outlying communities, and the church has built no ministry bridge to the new people in the community. It will die.

Old age, like ethnikitis, is terminal and also caused by local contextual factors. It is a disease not of a changing community but of a disintegrating community. Old age is mostly a rural disease while ethnikitis is mostly urban. Some rural communities are getting smaller and smaller, businesses are closing, and family farms are being taken over by large agricorporations. Churches in situations like this have little if any growth potential, and if the social process continues they will die. Notice that there is nothing the board of elders or the pastor can do about the conditions causing ethnikitis or old age, and therefore there is no reason for the church to feel guilty about its illness. It needs special care.

People-blindness occurs when churches do not recognize the important cultural differences which glue large social groups together and which can become barriers to the communication of the Good News. The notion that "our church can win anybody" is good rhetoric, but poor church growth thinking. God has given your church the ability to reach only a limited number and kind of people, and this you should be doing well. That is why I mentioned that, in writing a philosophy of ministry, you need to be explicit about the sociocultural profile of your congregation. While biblical ethics do not permit a church to develop a racist or segregationist philosophy of ministry, they do not prohibit narrowcasting the gospel and giving priority to certain market segments. At the same time, efforts need to be made to see that other churches are established which qualify for reaching each one of the segments of society. In that way the total body reaches the total population.

Hyper-cooperativism sets in when a church thinks its growth problem will be solved by joining a cooperative evangelistic program with other churches. An increasing body of research indicates that there is little direct relationship between cooperative evangelistic programs as we have known them and the growth of participating churches. Nothing can substitute for a good program of local church evangelism with the application of church growth principles. Hyper-cooperativism, however, is a curable disease, and some new models of cooperative evangelism now being experimented with may well point to a brighter future.

Koinonitis has been mentioned before as fellowship inflammation. When Christians develop *koinonia* or fellowship to such an exaggerated extent that all their attention and energies are being absorbed by other Christians, evangelistic myopia is likely to settle in. The lost are out there around the church, but they no longer are a high priority. Even when new people come into the church, the fellowship circles have been so rigidly defined that the new people cannot fit it. Strangers are a threat to churches with koinonitis.

Sociological strangulation afflicts only growing churches. It occurs when the physical facilities of the church can no longer accommodate the people flow. Sanctuary seating space is one of the vulnerable areas for strangulation. If in any regular service over 80 percent of the seats are taken, the church is already losing potential members. The other most vulnerable area is parking. At the peak traffic hour of the week there should be vacant spaces in the parking lot. If not and if the parking lot is full and overflowing, the church has a growth problem that needs to be solved.

Arrested spiritual development occurs in churches which are not well-fed with the Word of God. Since, as the Bible says, "God gives the increase," true church growth is ultimately God's work. But He ordinarily chooses to work through human instruments, and Christian people are the instruments that God uses to produce church growth. Unfortunately, however, in some churches the members are not suitable instruments for God to use. The spiritual level in those churches is very low. The church scores low on the quality scale. In some cases many members are not even born again. No wonder normal growth cannot occur.

Saint John's syndrome is named after the apostle John who wrote the book of Revelation and described the seven churches of Asia Minor. The churches were about forty years old and most had become nominal. Second generation churches which have not been adding new members regularly generally become very nominal and their growth slows down or stops. They are lukewarm and no longer receiving the vital blessing of God in growth.

If you suspect that your church might have one or more of these diseases, what can you do about it? For one thing, you can call in an expert just as you do when your physical body is sick. Church doctors are not as readily available as human doctors, but the number is growing rapidly. My colleague Carl F. George, who directs the Charles E. Fuller Institute of Evangelism and Church Growth, has developed the first professional-level training program for church growth consultants. He now oversees an expanding nationwide network of skilled consultants. These people know how to diagnose church illnesses and prescribe remedies if the disease is curable. They are still fairly expensive, but more and more churches are considering consultants' fees just another aspect of the price needed to pay for growth. If you want more information write to Carl F. George, Charles E. Fuller Institute of Evangelism and Church Growth, Dept. 352.230, P.O. Box 91990, Pasadena, California 91109-1990.

With the awareness that not every church can afford a consultant, the Fuller Institute has also developed a number of do-it-yourself diagnostic tools. The major one is an inexpensive *Diagnostic Clinic* that the pastor can use in guiding the lay leaders of the church through a self-diagnosis. This is keyed in my book *Your Church Can Be Healthy* (Abingdon Press, 1979), which I also recommend. These tools not only help you look at your church itself, but also help you analyze the growth potential in the surrounding community.

The Awesome Power of Setting Goals

If you have a church growth pastor in leadership position, if you know and believe in your philosophy of ministry, and if you have made a realistic diagnosis of the health of your church, you are ready to look to the future. What do you think God wants your church to be five years from now?

Asking this question may sound somewhat innocuous, but it is not. The overwhelming consensus of individuals whom God has blessed with large, growing churches is that it could never be done without the faith required to set goals. I agree with Arthur Adams who says, "Faith is the most important qualification of a leader. A commitment to something so strong that it shapes the leader's life is contagious."[3]

One of the most dynamic young pastors I know is Rick Warren, pastor of Saddleback Valley Community Church in Laguna Hills, California, whom I have mentioned previously. He founded his church on Easter Sunday, 1980, and has set a public goal of 20,000 members by the year 2020. That is his long-range goal, and every quarter he evaluates progress and sets short-range goals accordingly. The church is in its fourth year and is right on target. There were 1,000 in attendance on Easter of 1983, although, of course, average attendance is lower. Rick Warren is one of those persons who has the ability to analyze and verbalize what he does. He says, "The faith of the church is never larger than the vision of its pastor." For Warren, his principal responsibility is to dream of the future. "I can hire people with spiritual gifts I do not have," he says, "but I cannot delegate others to believe God for me." He dares to believe God for big things.

The world's largest church, pastored by Paul Yonggi Cho, is running over 300,000 members as I write this. His public goal is 500,000 members by the end of 1984, the centennial year of Christianity in Korea. Cho says, "The number one requirement for having real church growth—unlimited church growth—is to set goals."[4] He, of course, was not always the pastor of a large church. He started in a tent. But Cho says that early in his ministry, "God showed me the importance of setting goals and having faith to believe He would provide the growth for which I dreamed." The first year he asked for 150 members and got them. He set goals for doubling in each of the second and third years and did it, ending with 600. Then his faith grew enough to ask God for 3,000 within the next three years, and he reached the goal.[5] He now has faith large enough to trust God for one-half million.

Goal setting is a never-ending process. Faith builds faith. Robert Schuller says, "By all means, set goals *beyond* your goals. And if there are any obstacles in the way that would keep you from establishing larger goals, realize that these obstacles must be removed at any cost—or accept the fact that the seed of death and decay is already planted."[6] It is a sad day for many a church when the mortgage is burned and no more plans for expansion have been drawn.

Discovering the awesome power unlocked through the process of goal setting is one thing, but setting the goals is something else. Be sure that the goals you set are good goals. Test them against these five characteristics:

First, be sure your goals are relevant. They

must be the right goals. Insist that your evangelistic program, for example, has established goals of making disciples, not merely getting decisions for Christ. You will usually hit what you aim for. Furthermore, in order for goals to be relevant they have to be based on reality. A thorough diagnosis of the health of your church provides the basis on which to set relevant goals.

Second, your goals must be measurable. There is little value in setting some vague goal for which you do not have a measuring instrument. Then the measurement must be taken across a stated period of time. Every goal worth its salt includes a defined time frame. And finally there must be some system of accountability built into the process. This is a frequent problem area because it involves risk, but make sure that someone other than yourself will hold you accountable for attaining the goal when the time is up. Announcing the goal publicly as have Rick Warren and Paul Yonggi Cho is one of the best ways of assuring accountability.

Third, a good goal is significant. Shy away from meager goals and learn to trust God for the big things. At a crucial point in the development of the Church on the Way, pastor Jack Hayford received a special word from God. He felt, when he first accepted the call to the church, that he was being consigned to an obscure, tiny pastorate. Then God spoke to him directly as he was driving along the Hollywood Freeway and said, "You mustn't think too small, or you will get in My way; for I have set Myself to do a great work."[7] After that experience Hayford did not dare to think small. He set big goals and now pastors one of America's greatest churches. When the goal is significant enough to make a difference, not only the pastor but the people feel their faith stretched and strengthened.

Fourth, but the goal also must be manageable. This balances out the significance factor and helps us understand that a goal must not be obviously out of reach. Coming up with pipe dreams and setting ridiculous goals is counterproductive and produces so much frustration that some people who do it no longer want to practice goal setting. But don't carry this one so far that you deal with trivia. It is better to attempt something great and fail than attempt nothing and succeed. Elmer Towns tells that some years ago pastor Jerry Falwell of Thomas Road Baptist Church in Lynchburg, Virginia, was bold enough to set a goal for 12,000 in Sunday School. The goal was not reached, and Falwell said, "This is the first time I've ever apologized for 9,172 in Sunday school."[8]

Finally, good goals are personal. Make sure that you have goal ownership on the part of those whose efforts are essential for the fulfillment of the goal. All too many pastors have set goals that they believe in, but their people don't, and the goals, of course, are shipwrecked. You can test the level of goal ownership by measuring the people's commitment of time, money, or energy to its accomplishment. This is crucial and all the gifts and skills of leadership described in other sections of this book will need to be employed to make sure it happens.

Most church leaders can set goals according to these principles without much problem. Those who would like some additional help, however, may want to know about a couple of resources. First of all, the *Diagnostic Clinic* produced by the Fuller Institute (Dept. 352-230, P.O. Box 91990, Pasadena, California 91109-1990) which I mentioned earlier is designed to stimulate a goal-setting exercise with goal ownership built into the process. Many churches have found it extremely helpful. A second resource is a workbook that Bob Waymire and I have compiled called *The Church Growth Survey Handbook.* It will help you do some significant diagnosis of your church and then take you step by step through making faith projections for growth. It is available for $3.50 plus postage from Global Church Growth, P.O. Box 66, Santa Clara, California 95052.

Notes

1. Lyle E. Schaller, *The Pastor and the People* (Nashville: Abingdon Press, 1973), p. 27.

2. The designations "classroom church" and "life-situation church" are taken from *All Originality Makes a Dull Church* by Dan Baumann (Ventura, CA: Vision House, 1976) an excellent book which unfortunately is now out of print and unavailable.

3. Arthur Merrihew Adams, *Effective Leadership for Today's Church* (Philadelphia: Westminster Press, 1978), p. 1.

4. Paul Yonggi Cho, *Successful Home Cell Groups* (Plainfield, NJ: Logos International, 1981), p. 162.

5. *Ibid.*, p. 2.

6. Robert H. Schuller, *Your Church Has Real Possibilities* (Ventura, CA: Regal Books, 1974), p. 83.

7. Jack W. Hayford, *The Church on the Way* (Lincoln, VA: Chosen Books, 1982), p. 24.

8. Elmer L. Towns, *America's Fastest Growing Churches* (Nashville: Impact Books, 1972), p. 205.

7

Keeping Growth on Course

This final chapter is addressed to pastors, but laypeople will profit from reading it also. Assuming that the pieces are in place for growth, that the steps outlined in the last chapter have been taken, and that some growth has started, I have selected seven areas that pastors need to keep their finger on in order to build and sustain growth momentum. There are more than seven areas that could be mentioned and much more could be said about each one. But I have long since learned that it is impossible to say it all in any one book, so I have tried to be very selective and to choose the areas of highest priority.

The Pastor as Change Agent

I was somewhat surprised to see some recent research on the way American pastors relate to church programming, but the more I ponder it the more realistic it seems. The research concludes that 5 percent of American pastors *invent*. They are creative and can design their own programs.

Another 15 percent *adapt*. They are innovative and have the ability to take principles and programs that someone else comes up with and tailor them to fit their particular situation. But then a full 80 percent of pastors *adopt*. They are not particularly interested in making up their own programs or introducing changes in an existing program. They have only the time and ability to implement a program that is handed to them with little or no change and many of them can implement it very skillfully. In my church growth classes and writings I try to help pastors move from the 80 percent of adopters to the 15 percent of adapters. The inventors are a breed apart.

Pastors who attempt to apply church growth principles to their churches function as change agents. That means they are faced with a social group (the congregation) which over the years has developed certain traditions of church life. These traditions to one degree or another have become part of their self-identity. Some of them are considerably difficult to change, but they need to be changed in order for the church to grow. How do you make this happen?

Repeating what I have said before, the indispensable first step in guiding a church through change is earning the right to lead the people. This is done by proving to them that you are their servant, and it typically takes three to six years, although it can happen sooner. Large doses of patience, love, sensitivity and persistence are called for at this stage. Once you are accepted as the leader, you are then in a position to introduce innovation. For each major change, however, you will need to take at least four steps.

First, share your vision. The vision for where God wants the church to go usually is channeled through the pastor. While there are exceptions to this, it has been the case in virtually every study of church growth that I have made. But to be effective, the vision must be communicated to the people in a way that will excite them and motivate them to do their part toward making it a reality. The appropriate channels of communication vary from church to church, but the pulpit is a constant. However the pulpit is so powerful that you need to make sure the groundwork has been properly laid before announcing your goals. Many pastors have taken a year to prepare the way for a pulpit announcement on a major innovation such as a sanctuary building program. Bulletins and newsletters are commonly used, but there is no substitute for a vision which has gripped the pastor so overwhelmingly that everyone who comes into contact with him or her is bound to catch part of the vision. Visions are caught more than taught.

Second, accumulate feedback. There is wisdom in a multitude of counselors. If God has given you the vision, it will usually be in embryonic form and needs a great deal of detailed refinement and development before it can become a reality. Here is where you need the counsel of your people. Not only do you need their ideas, but you need them to feel like the vision is theirs also, and for some people this means having an opportunity to contribute their ideas for whatever they are worth. So give a high priority to opening channels for feedback.

I have previously mentioned my friend, Kent Tucker, pastor of Grace Church, Aurora, Colorado. He is a skillful change agent. I have been able to observe in detail the excellent feedback-producing mechanisms that he created when a decision was needed for moving ahead on new facilities, both temporary and permanent. Over a period of seven weeks, Tucker distributed a one- to four-page position paper from himself to the whole congregation on Sunday mornings. Each one contained a response device which said: "What is your response? We want and need your input." By the end of the two-month period, Tucker not only had the benefit of some fine ideas from his people, but he also had the people with him because they felt that they had personally contributed to the plans for growth. But this was not all. Kent Tucker made sure that, during the process, he had made personal contact through breakfast and luncheon engagements with all the persons in the church he could identify as opinion formers. They included those who were in official church positions and also those who exercised their influence through informal networks of relationships in the church.

Third, promote harmony in the body. As a change agent you must realize that the people of your congregation will fall along a spectrum from radicals through progressives and conservatives to traditionalists at the other extreme. Knowing into which category the people you are dealing with fall, will help you decide which kind of approach to take. You need to cool the radicals down a little. If you don't, they will push you so hard and so fast that it will disrupt the harmony of the whole group. The progressives are your natural allies. They are in favor of moderate change. The conservatives will keep you from moving too fast. They will permit change, but not easily. They will help you sharpen your reasons for doing what you are doing. The traditionalists, who oppose change of any kind, can be your biggest problem. You should do your best to win them over, but if you cannot you will either have to live with their "no" vote or in some cases reconcile yourself to the fact that they need to move on to another church because they are obstructing congregational harmony. This is frequently a very difficult and painful position to take.

Fourth, discern the proper timing. There is no formula for knowing when to take the crucial congregational vote or make a key announcement from the pulpit. It is something which only can be felt. It is an intuition which comes from God, and for this reason a great deal of prayer should be invested at this point. When you know you have obtained goal ownership from the people, you have your best clue to move ahead. If the people feel part of the change process, and if they have truly caught the vision, you can then mobilize them to make the contributions of time, energy, and money necessary for the change to take place.

As the change process goes forward, you will also want to be planning action in these seven areas which are crucial components of building and sustaining growth momentum.

Pray for More Faith

In 1977 pastor Al Henson graduated from Liberty Baptist Seminary in Lynchburg, Virginia. While there he stood out among the students as a person of prayer and faith. Even before he went to seminary, God had called him to plant a new church in Nashville, Tennessee, so he prayed for this all three years he was in seminary. After graduation Al Henson and his wife moved to Nashville and began services in the recreation room of the apartment complex where they lived. They began with a congregation of 41, and the church grew to 1,000 in five years. One of the chief reasons for the growth of this church, called Lighthouse Baptist

Church, was serious and sustained prayer.

Elmer L. Towns tells that when the church was only two months old, Henson was driving down Interstate 24 and passed a piece of property which he claimed for the church. The owner flatly refused to sell, so Henson went back, walked the property line and prayed for the property. Then the Lord impressed him to fast for three days, praying that God would touch the heart of the owner. After he did, he visited the owner once more and shared his vision for winning Nashville to Christ. The next day the owner called Henson and said, "The Lord spoke to me as I have never had Him speak to me before. I know that God wants you to have this property." But he tacked on some stringent financial requirements which were met during the next ninety days only by other obviously miraculous touches of God's hand.[1]

My interpretation of the dynamics of that case study is that without Pastor Henson's special time of prayer and fasting, Lighthouse Baptist Church today would not be anywhere near 1,000 in attendance. Prayer is a growth factor which has not been stressed nearly enough in church growth literature. All the facts are not yet known, but it seems that most American pastors are surprisingly low in their ministry of prayer. One study shows them averaging one hour a week, which figures out to between eight or nine minutes per day.[2] The average Korean pastor, who spends from one to three hours a day in prayer, would be appalled. We have a great deal to learn.

One of the areas that could be stressed profitably in American churches is biblical fasting. Without doubt there are some spiritual dynamics released through fasting that otherwise remain dormant. Paul Yonggi Cho says, "In fact, 90 percent of the prayers that have resulted in definite answers in our church have been those prayers that have been combined with fasting."[3] Many members of Full Gospel Central Church in Seoul, Korea, regularly fast one day per week. Occasionally some do it for three days, some have fasted fifteen to twenty days, and a few have followed the example of Jesus and fasted forty days.

I suggest that as you fast and pray, you ask God to take you to a higher level of faith. I see Christian faith activated at four levels, with most of us located on levels one and two.

The first level of faith is saving faith. Believing in Jesus for salvation is the first step of the Christian life. "For by grace you have been saved through faith" (Eph. 2:8).

The second level is sanctifying faith. Faith is the fruit of the Spirit, a quality of Christian life to be continually cultivated. Second-level faith gives the Christian special strength for holy living and power for witnessing. For most of my Christian life I didn't know there were any more levels available to today's Christians.

The third level of faith, as I now see it, is possibility thinking faith. I have taken the name from the teachings of pastor Robert Schuller because I learned it from him. It is goal-setting faith. It is putting substance on things hoped for as we read in Hebrews 11:1. It is the faith I described when I talked about setting goals in the last chapter. It is the faith of Al Henson of Lighthouse Baptist Church. Here are Schuller's own words: "Possibility thinking is the maximum utilization of the God-given powers of imagination exercised in dreaming up possible ways by which a desired objective can be attained." He goes on to say that it is the kind of faith Jesus referred to when He mentioned speaking to a mountain and seeing it move.[4]

The fourth level of faith I call fourth dimension faith, taking the name from the title of one of Paul Yonggi Cho's books, *The Fourth Dimension* (Logos International, 1979). This is the faith which trusts God for supernatural signs and wonders. It is the "shield of faith" which withstands principalities, powers, and the rulers of darkness of this age as described in Ephesians 6:10-17. This level of faith has become tangible to me through a course that I have helped Pastor John Wimber teach in Fuller Seminary, beginning in 1982, called "MC510: Signs, Wonders and Church Growth." Not only has God shown us signs and wonders directly in the classroom, but our research has begun to uncover previously hidden facts about how this fourth level of faith relates to the growth of the church.[5] This is especially true of the origins of many of our present-day denominations. My perception is that many more of us will be intimately acquainted with the fourth level of faith before the end of the decade of the eighties. If so, our churches will most likely grow as never before.

Be Prepared to Solve Problems

Having a vision for growth does not mean you will be free from problems. However as faith builds, problems will be seen more and more as opportunities. If you intend to lead your church to growth, you should plan to budget a considerable portion of your time for trouble-shooting and problem-solving. If you are the leader, the buck will need to stop with you.

Having clear goals will help solve problems. One secret is to recognize a problem in its early stages before it gets out of hand, and once it is recognized, do not postpone tackling it, unpleasant as the thought may be. One way to do this is continually to monitor your progress, setting and resetting short-range goals. Mid-course corrections are extremely important to keep you from losing hard-earned growth momentum.

The Church Growth Movement has always stressed pragmatism, and still does even though many have criticized it. It is not the kind of pragmatism that comprises doctrine or ethics or the kind that dehumanizes people by using them as means toward an end. It is, however, the kind of consecrated pragmatism which ruthlessly examines traditional methodologies and programs asking the tough questions. If some sort of ministry in the church is not reaching intended goals, consecrated pragmatism says there is something wrong which needs to be corrected.

Let me refer once again to pastor Rick Warren of Saddleback Valley Community Church. I love his consecrated pragmatism. He is a leader who has clear goals and who will not allow anyone to use "we never did it that way before" as an excuse for inaction, mediocrity, or inertia. In order to understand this it is necessary to realize that Rick Warren is a Southern Baptist. Of all American denominations, Southern Baptists are in a very high percentile of those with the most rigid traditions. Warren is a loyal supporter of the denominational traditions—except where they may become obstacles to church growth. There are at least four hallowed traditions he boldly ignores which rather shocks many denominational colleagues.

First, Warren chose not to use the name "Baptist" in the name of his church. It is thoroughly Baptist in polity and practice, but the name is

Saddleback Valley Community Church. Warren discovered that the name "Baptist" is not particularly appealing in Southern California. If his church were in South Carolina, he would certainly call it "Baptist"—he has nothing personally against the name.

Second, the Southern Baptist tradition is that the Sunday School serves as the cutting edge of the church's evangelistic efforts. This may not be the best way to approach the population living in and around Laguna Hills, however. So Warren has made space advertising and direct mail advertising the central thrust of evangelism. Over 40 percent of the new members of his church first heard of it through advertising.

Third, almost every Southern Baptist church gives a public invitation for salvation, rededication, baptism and church membership after every service. Warren discovered that this was offensive to some of the unchurched people in his area of South Orange County. So he never gives an invitation except to ask people to fill out a response envelope and leave it there or mail it in later. The results are as good as the best of the traditional type invitations.

Fourth, the traditional procedure for taking out membership in a Southern Baptist church is one of the nation's easiest. If you have been baptized as a believer, you can go up after any service and take out membership on the spot. Rick Warren, a student of church growth, had learned the principle of commitment which I have explained elsewhere. So he requires a six-week class for new members, and has discovered that raising the commitment level is in fact a practical growth principle.

Plan Effective Outreach

Your church has good news for the people of your community. Therefore, you must constantly check to see that you are using the best methods of communicating that message to the unchurched people around you. What can you do to be sure you are?

First, learn from experience. It is fine to experiment with some new methodology of outreach, but test it to be sure it works. Don't be like the pastor that Monica Hill, editor of the British *Church Growth Digest*, tells about. This pastor reported that he had mobilized some of his people to knock on doors with Christian literature as an evangelistic outreach method. The first quarter they knocked on 2,000 doors. "What was the response?" asked Monica Hill. "How many meaningful contacts did you make?" The pastor's answer: "None—so we are going to redouble our efforts. We will knock on 4,000 doors next quarter!"

Second, know the felt needs of the unchurched in your community. There is one fairly simple and effective way to do this. Take an opinion poll of at least 100 households in your ministry area. Select the sample as carefully as you can, attempting to match the households you visit roughly with your own congregation in terms of ethnicity, socioeconomic status, educational level, age, and geographical proximity. Knock on the doors and ask them for their opinion—most will be glad to give it to you. Then ask Rick Warren's five questions (which he has adapted from questions that Robert Schuller used years ago):

1. *Are you an active member of a nearby church?* If the answer is yes, the interview stops there. Wish the person well, but remember that

you are looking for the opinion of *unchurched.*

2. *What do you think is the greatest need in* (insert the name of your area or community)?

3. *Why do you think most people don't attend church?* Be sure you don't change the wording of this key question.

4. *If you were looking for a church in the area, what kinds of things would you look for?*

5. *What advice would you give me as the pastor of a nearby church? What, for example, could I do for you?*

Take notes as you talk, then leave the person a brochure describing your church. When you have 100 pages of notes, study them for a long time in an attitude of prayer. You should find you have a good handle on the felt needs of the unchurched in your area.

The third suggestion I have is to target your outreach on the responsive. Don't be haphazard, but be systematic as to how you invest the human effort and energy in outreach. Resistance-receptivity theory, a prominent part of church growth teaching through the years, attempts to discover ways of predicting ahead of time which groups of people will be more receptive to the message of the Good News. Here are some well-tested hints:

Start with friends and relatives of church members, especially friends and relatives of new converts. Many call this *oikos* (Greek for household) evangelism, and it works well.

Start with new arrivals in the community. It may take some persistent research to discover how you can identify these people, but your efforts will pay handsomely. There usually is a way.

Start with visitors to your church. Give high priority to making contact, within a day or so, with all those who live in your ministry area and visit your church or Sunday School.

Start with people whose needs you can meet. The opinion poll that you have taken is designed to inform you of the spectrum of needs. Carefully decide which ones your church can specialize in and strive for excellence in those areas.

Start with people who are passing through a critical period in their lives and who need a special touch of love and concern.

Two pastor friends recently did some very creative things in order to develop points of contact with unchurched in their area, both focusing initially on children. One in Denver held a "kids' fair" in a neighborhood school. It was a festive time designed around all kinds of booths and games with darts and beanbags and wet sponges and bottles. At the fair each child was invited to have his or her picture taken with a likeness of E.T. Afterwards, members of a ministry team from the church hand-delivered the developed pictures to the parents and talked to them about the church and about Jesus Christ.

My other friend, in northern Pennsylvania, hired an artist to paint a mural on a church wall. It depicted Jesus blessing the children. A ministry team from the church then went through the neighborhood asking parents if they would like their child painted with Jesus. Those who did took their boys and girls to pose for the artist and in each case a meaningful contact was made with a new family. In both cases these churches were doing the children a favor and the parents appreciated it.

Assimilate New Members

Many churches with active outreach ministries find that they still do not grow well. Baptisms are high. Many new members come into the church. But attendance remains constant from one year to the next. This state of affairs is usually a symptom of a weakness in the assimilation process. The back door of the church is wide open, and you need to take steps to shut it.

Generally speaking there are two major ways to make sure a new member becomes assimilated. One is assigning a task. If individuals find themselves with a responsibility which contributes to the well-being of the church, it is likely they will stay. As the church grows, however, it becomes more and more difficult to assign church tasks to new members. In larger churches most openings for tasks are found in the face-to-face fellowship groups. Creating such groups is the second major way that new members can be assimilated.

One of the most serious growth-inhibiting attitudes that develops in a church is what Lyle Schaller calls "their natural inclination to think of their congregation as 'one big family.' "[6] Of course small, single-cell churches have already decided that they are and will remain one family and that is why their growth potential is so low.

One of the seven vital signs of a healthy church listed in my book *Your Church Can Grow* (Regal Books, 1976) is the proper balance between what I call the celebration, the congregation, and the cell. The celebration is the worship service where all the members of the church gather to meet with God. The basic function of the *celebration* is worship, although other things happen as well. Any number can join in worship, in some cases the more the better. The *congregation's* basic function is to provide meaningful social fellowship for the members. It is a face-to-face group, and can best produce this fellowship when it is between about thirty-five and eighty members. The *cell's* function is more than face-to-face, it brings people into a heart-to-heart relationship producing a high level of personal intimacy and accountability. The optimum size for cell groups is eight to twelve.

While there are some exceptions to this in certain situations (such as areas of low social mobility where extended families live in the same area), in most urban and suburban settings, developing groups like these will be a key to assimilating your new members. It is imperative for church growth pastors to supervise this rigidly. Ideally, the groups themselves should have such a vision for growth that they voluntarily initiate the formation of new groups on a regular basis. Realistically, however, this rarely happens. As I have mentioned, *koinonia* all too easily becomes koinonitis, and face-to-face groups may actually oppose change. Only persistently strong top-level leadership can initiate and continue the process of new group formation.

There are times when the group structure of a church is very subtle. I know of one large church that has been losing young adults primarily because of its group structure. The church assumes that high school graduates will go on to college, so the college class is designed to provide group fellowship for them. Because of the natural snobbishness of college students, those high school graduates who choose to move directly into the job market are effectively excluded. No group in the church has been created to meet the needs of eighteen- to twenty-five-year-olds who are working, so many of them slip out the back door, unnoticed by the pastoral staff. To create a college-career class would not be the solution. The college class is part of the *youth* department and rightly so. But working people perceive themselves to be adults, so a class for them should be part of the *adult* department even though they are the same age as those in the college group.

It is helpful if the leaders and members of the congregations or face-to-face groups can understand their responsibility to assimilate new members. I like the model that my friend pastor Frank Barker of Briarwood Presbyterian Church in Birmingham, Alabama has established. As this goes to press they are running 2,500 in attendance. Twelve elders of the church have been assigned the responsibility of "tribe leader" and placed over a geographical area. Within each tribe area are several "flocks," each shepherded by an "area presbyter" who reports to the tribe leader. A detailed *Shepherding Manual* prepared by Barker himself sets forth the requirements to contact every member of the group at least once a month and to hold regular flock meetings to promote fellowship. Then it says, "Be responsible for the assimilation of new members assigned to your area." When a person from the area enrolls in the new-member class at the church, the area presbyter is called in on the fourth Sunday of the six-week class. The new member is introduced to the area presbyter who goes over the material in the new-member packet with him or her. The area presbyter is to find out about the new member's interests and spiritual gifts and explain the various avenues of service that the church offers. The area presbyter is also responsible to see that the new member becomes part of a home Bible study group and the Sunday School. No wonder the back door remains closed in Briarwood Presbyterian Church.

Notice that the shepherding system at Briarwood can only operate as Frank Barker functions as a rancher, not a shepherd. His church is very happy with this arrangement. Likewise the Full Gospel Central Church in Seoul, Korea. Paul Yonggi Cho says, "In our church it is impossible for me to have personal contact with all 150,000 members [now 300,000 at this writing]. But through the cell leaders I do have contact in a secondary way with them. I am assured that our members are properly cared for, properly disciplined, properly fed—and properly corrected when needed."[7] I agree with Lyle Schaller who says, "The responsibility of the rancher or bishop is to see the total picture, to make sure that everything gets done, rather than attempt to do all the work singlehandedly."[8] Part of seeing the whole picture is making sure new members are assimilated into the life of your church.

Nurture the Homesteaders

In a previous chapter I mentioned the predictable pioneer-homesteader conflict which has caught many a pastor unawares. Knowing about it and understanding it for what it is constitutes an important first step in managing the conflict for growth. I cannot count how many pastors have shared their pioneer-homesteader conflict with me, and I am sorry to report that the majority were defeated by it.

The pioneers, who are the old guard, have identified a set of traditions and customs, "our way of doing things," with the church itself. If the church is plateaued for a period of time these traditions become more deeply entrenched every year. Of course there is no conflict over that period of time because there is no threat to the traditions. But then if a plateaued church begins to grow for any number of reasons, such as a revival, the pastor acquiring church growth "eyes," a new pastor oriented to growth, or what have you, trouble may be just around the corner.

The conflict usually does not surface as soon as the church begins to grow. Pioneers at first are delighted to see new members. But as the growth continues and as the new members begin to feel more comfortable in the congregation, the pioneers begin to gain an awareness that their control will soon be threatened. They expected that new members would adopt the values and behavior patterns of the pioneers, and they are disturbed when the reality dawns that many of the homesteaders have quite different agendas.

One of the most helpful analyses that I have seen of the pioneer-homesteader conflict comes from pastor Richard Hertel of Ridgeview Hill Christian Reformed Church near Denver. He points out that "pioneer disaffection is often highly emotional." While issues are identified and apparently addressed rationally, these are often a facade covering the real feelings. Hertel says, "After a recent series of meetings at Ridgeview Hills with a group of upset pioneers, it became apparent that the real concerns were neither theological nor cognitive." The pioneers were really afraid that "we were losing our 'Christian Reformedness.' " They had Dutch heritage and their families had gone back for generations in the denomination. The church and its traditions had become part of the fabric of their personal self-identity. In four years of growth under Hertel the congregation had gone from 80 percent Dutch down to barely 50 percent, and it is easy to see how this could arouse emotions.

The pioneers were right. Traditions were indeed changing. "Under these conditions," Hertel says, "the pastor should once more lay out the vision, embrace the persons, and invite them to join the pilgrimage." Sometimes the pioneers can be won over, not usually by well-seasoned presentations in board meetings, but by intense one-on-one nurturing or a visitation of the Holy Spirit in genuine renewal which melts hearts and cements relationships. But sometimes, as Hertel says, "the most pastoral act may be to help such members find a new church home."[9] That, of course, is the last resort. But whatever the course of action, the end result should be placing the homesteaders into the functional (not just formal) lay leadership circles of the church.

I was glad to hear of an unusually happy outcome of a potential pioneer-homesteader conflict from my friend pastor Don Baker of Hinson Memorial (Baptist) Church in Portland, Oregon. He has been pastor for nine years and seen membership grow from 800 to 2,800, with 300 additional members being sent off to plant new churches. Of the 2,800 present members, 2,700 are homesteaders, persons who came in since he took the pastorate.

When Baker first went to Hinson Memorial he had an advantage because he had served as an assistant on the staff some years previously. He knew ahead of time who the de facto leader of the pioneers was, and he knew this man was inherently opposed to change. So he arranged to have lunch with him once a week from 12:00 to 2:00. He poured his life into him and developed a close rapport over the months. He invited him to staff meetings and spent weekends with the family. Then, at the proper time, Don Baker invited his pioneer friend, who had traditionally been against expansion, to become the church's Director of Expansion at a salary of $1 per year. He accepted and became the up-front person in the entire decision-making process. Needless to say, he carried not only the homesteaders but also his fellow pioneers, and the church has grown at a decadal rate of 302 percent.

Add the Staff You Need

Most churches are understaffed for growth. They are staffed for maintenance and survival, but not for growth. If your church is to sustain growth momentum, staffing must become a very high priority. Before I make a few commments on staffing for growth, let me recommend the best book on the subject: Lyle E. Schaller's *The Multiple Staff and the Larger Church* (Abingdon Press, 1980). If there is any question on the part of either clergy or laity about when and how to add staff, this book should provide the answers.

In a growing church both the quantity and the quality of the staff is important. The rule of thumb for quantity is that you should have a program staff person (plus backup personnel such as secretaries) for each 100 active members. This sounds like too many because most churches are understaffed for growth. In my church planting classes I recommend that a church which plans to move past the 200 barrier should ideally start with a senior pastor and one staff member. If this is impossible, add the new staff member before the church gets to 100 active members and another before it gets to 200. At this stage of growth, investment in staff is much wiser than investment in facilities. Use rental facilities much longer than you think you should. When pastor Jack Hayford began his ministry in Church on the Way, 24 people attended the first service. He immediately added two staff people and the growth of that church is now a living legend.[10] Pastor Kent Tucker started Grace Church, Aurora, Colorado with two staff and added a third before the active membership reached 200. Not every church is the same, and there are other variables which enter the picture, but this is a good rule of thumb.

As to staff quality, I have three suggestions:

First, recruit new staff on the basis of spiritual gifts. When a pastor asks me, "What staff person should I add next?" they usually expect me to say a minister of music or a youth minister or a minister of outreach. I never say that. I say that they should find a person who has spiritual gifts which they don't have. Just like the Body of Christ as a whole, the program staff should be a team made up of persons whose abilities complement each other rather than overlap. The ideal of the omni-competent pastor is a negative growth factor. I agree with Lyle Schaller who criticizes denominations and educational systems which "are designed to encourage ministers to attend continuing education events in those areas of ministry where they don't do very well." He goes on to say, "Pick out what you do best and do it."[11] When all members of the staff are working in their areas of giftedness you can expect maximum harmony, job satisfaction, and effectiveness of ministry.

Second, recruit new staff on the basis of devotion to the senior pastor. From Max Weber on, theoreticians have underscored the need for staff loyalty to the charismatic leader. From this perspective it seems almost incredible that at one point early in its development, the consistory of Robert Schuller's Crystal Cathedral (then called Garden Grove Community Church) hired an associate for Schuller while he was on vacation and without his knowledge. Needless to say, not only the associate but the consistory were soon changed. Paul Yonggi Cho employs a unique system to take care of staff members who decide they want to be senior pastors. He says, "I will provide him with a salary and enough expense money to start his own church elsewhere." As of 1980, seventy-five churches had been started in that way.[12]

Finally, be sure the new staff members heartily buy into the philosophy of ministry of the church. This is another reason for going through the process of putting your philosophy of ministry in writing. This should not be just intellectual consent, but a heartfelt conviction. When they join the staff they should feel like they are joining a cause.

One way that some churches have found helpful in obtaining all three of the above qualities is to recruit new staff from the congregation itself. I am aware of a number of large churches such as First Baptist Church, Modesto, California, under pastor Bill Yaeger, and Grace Community Church of the Valley in Panorama City, California, under pastor John MacArthur, which have recruited virtually their whole staff from members of the congregation. Nationwide I see it as a small-scale trend. The advantages are obvious. The candidate's spiritual gifts are well-known and there is no question about loyalty to the senior pastor or buy-in to the philosophy of ministry.

The frontrunner in adapting Paul Yonggi Cho's system of home cell groups to the American scene may be pastor Norman Boschoff of Hoffmantown Baptist Church (Southern Baptist) near Albuquerque, New Mexico. He has also instituted one of the most aggressive and innovative staff recruiting programs I have seen. He invites any member of the church to try out to become a neighborhood group leader. Part of the dynamic of these neighborhood groups is that they must give birth constantly to new groups. If you are a successful group leader and if you become the spiritual parent of a total of sixteen groups, you then become eligible for a part-time position on the church staff with a salary of $2,900 annually (1983 dollars). As you add groups your salary goes up to $22,000 for thirty-two groups and a full-time staff position. Seminary graduates are encouraged to join the church and work themselves into a position, but their degrees won't do it for them. Only the fruit of their ministry will get them the job.

Preach for Growth

We have shelves of books on homiletics, but relatively little literature on how to preach specifically for church growth. I am looking forward to much more research on this in the future, but meanwhile I have five brief suggestions.

First, match your preaching to your philosophy of ministry. One of the advantages of writing out your church's philosophy of ministry is that it gives you direction in your preaching schedule. Obviously you will preach one way in a classroom church and another in a life-situation church. As you do your long-range planning and also as you prepare each sermon, have a clear idea as to whom you are addressing your thoughts. Then be consistent. Do not direct your message to one audience one Sunday and another the next, although this can be done in different services. Some churches have been successful in holding two Sunday morning worship services, each with a different style for a different audience. Others have found that their philosophy of ministry requires identical services. Some preach to unbelievers on

Sunday morning and believers on Sunday night. My point is that your philosophy of ministry is the starting point for clear thinking about preaching for growth.

Second, use the power of the pulpit to motivate your people for growth. Pastor Joe Harding of Central United Presbyterian Church (United Methodist), Richland, Washington, has seen his attendance soar to 1,200 in recent years. One of the reasons for this is that his people want the church to grow and are willing to pay the price. Harding agrees that the vision for growth starts with the pastor and that it must then be communicated to the congregation. "How does the congregation really know the pastor wants the church to grow?" Harding asks. "He proclaims it Sunday after Sunday from the pulpit. His messages lift up the priority of the Great Commission of Jesus Christ." Over a period of time the people catch the vision. "They begin to see the community through 'church growth eyes.' "[13]

Third, be positive. The gospel is good news, so make your sermons communicate good news. Be affirming and uplifting. Skillful preachers can even preach against sin in a positive way as Jesus illustrated when He was confronted with the woman taken in adultery and when He spoke to Zacchaeus. Robert Schuller counsels preachers to stimulate the positive emotions of the listeners such as "love, joy, peace, kindness, gentleness, faith, hope, humor, aspiration, trust, respect, self-confidence, enthusiasm, ambition, courage, optimism." He recommends not playing to the negative emotions such as "fear, suspicion, anger, prejudice, sorrow, despair, self-hate, pessimism."[14]

Fourth, avoid controversial topics. I am aware

that a suggestion to avoid controversial topics is itself a controversial topic. Some philosophies of ministry, such as Riverside Church in New York City, require the minister to deal with controversial topics from the pulpit. However, by and large, with notable but rare exceptions, controversial preaching is an antigrowth factor. This has been confirmed by an impressive body of research on the reasons for mainline church decline in the U.S.A. over the past two decades. American people, believers and unbelievers, are battered enough with controversy over the course of an average week. They come to church for a word of love, encouragement, and assurance.

Notice that the definition of what is or is not a controversial topic is determined by the profile of the congregation and its philosophy of ministry. Among Jerry Falwell's people, for example, abortion or allowing prayer in public schools are not controversial topics since he has 100 percent congregational consensus on the issues. In many other situations, however, they might be extremely controversial.

Finally, preach to personal needs. Use the opinion poll I have suggested as a starting point for discovering needs. Once you begin, your mental awareness will become programmed to pick up many more, and sermon topics will multiply. People need help and you can give it to them in your sermons. Use titles that are in the language of the people. Go to the newsstand and look over the titles of the articles of the best-selling magazines. Paul Yonggi Cho says, "People are always coming to church in great need, but if the preacher is only talking about theology, history and politics, the people are not going to be helped in their present lives where they need the message."[15] Keep your messages biblical, but keep them simple if you want to meet human need. I like the way Rick Warren once put it, "It's a sin to take the most exciting book in the world and bore people with it."

If you can serve a diet of positive sermons focused on the real, felt needs of the people you will be preaching for growth.

Notes

1. Elmer L. Towns, *An Analysis of the Gift of Faith in Church Growth* (Doctor of Ministry dissertation, Pasadena, CA: Fuller Theological Seminary, 1983), pp. 88-89.

2. Merrill E. Douglas and Joyce McNally, "How Ministers Use Their Time," *The Christian Ministry*, January 1980, p. 23.

3. Paul Yonggi Cho, *Successful Home Cell Groups* (Plainfield, NJ: Logos International, 1981), p. 133.

4. Robert H. Schuller, *Your Church Has Real Possibilities* (Ventura, CA: Regal Books, 1974), p. 86.

5. For more information on MC510: Signs, Wonders and Church Growth, order the study book *Signs and Wonders Today* from Christian Life, 396 E. St. Charles Rd., Wheaton, IL 60187. Send $4.95 plus $1.00 for postage and handling.

6. Lyle E. Schaller, *Growing Plans* (Nashville: Abingdon Press, 1983), p. 93.

7. Cho, *Successful Home Cell Groups*, p. 71.

8. Schaller, *Growing Plans*, p. 93.

9. Richard A. Hertel, "Pioneers and Homesteaders: Settling an Old Boundary Dispute" (Doctor of Ministry paper, Pasadena: Fuller Theological Seminary, 1982), p. 29.

10. See Jack W. Hayford, *The Church on the Way* (Santa Ana: Chosen Books, 1982), pp. 11,16.

11. "The Changing Focus of Church Finances," interview with Lyle E. Schaller, *Leadership*, Spring, 1981, p. 15.

12. Cho, *Successful Home Cell Groups*, p. 47.

13. Joe A. Harding, *Have I Told You Lately . . . ?* (Pasadena, CA: Church Growth Press, 1982), p. 13.

14. Schuller, *Your Church Has Real Possibilities*, p. 136.

15. Cho, *Successful Home Cell Groups*, p. 156.

Index